mini
Hong Kong
The Essential **Visitors'** Guide

Hong Kong mini Explorer
ISBN 13 – 978-976-8182-81-4
ISBN 10 – 976-8182-81-4

Copyright © Explorer Group Ltd 2007
All rights reserved.

All maps © Explorer Group Ltd 2007

Front cover photograph – Pete Maloney

Printed and bound by
Emirates Printing Press, Dubai, UAE

Explorer Publishing & Distribution
PO Box 34275, Zomorrodah Building,
Za'abeel Rd, Dubai, United Arab Emirates
Phone (+971 4) 335 3520 **Fax** (+971 4) 335 3529
Email info@explorerpublishing.com
Web www.explorerpublishing.com

The Hong Kong Mini Explorer is a pocket-sized parcel of essential information that will help you make the most of your trip to this fascinating part of the world. Within these pages you'll find everything from ancient temples to swanky bars. Written by Hong Kong residents, this mini marvel is brought to you by the same team responsible for the *Hong Kong Explorer: The Complete Residents' Guide*. If you want to know more about what we do, or tell us what we've missed, go to www.explorerpublishing.com.

The Explorer Team

Contents

Essentials

King Kong

Few places on the planet have developed as fast or as frantically as Hong Kong; fewer still have its curious mix of old and new world charms.

This meeting place of cultures and civilizations continues to defy simple description. Many have tried to define Hong Kong – Pearl of the Orient, Asia's World City and the City of Life – but no one has come close to the real thing.

Seen from afar, Hong Kong is a compact place crammed full of skyscrapers, chaotic streets and reminders of its mixed parentage. Frantic and densely populated, the downtown areas do little to dispel this, but dig deeper and Hong Kong's array of cultural and natural attractions will delight.

It is an undeniably modern and commercial place, but it's also one full of breathtaking beauty, some of which isn't immediately obvious. There is a wonder to the many contradictions that you'll see on the street, where identikit western architecture nestles next to ancient temples still serving a steady stream of locals seeking guidance.

On the surface lay the more obvious charms of the mountainous New Territories, the urban open space of Victoria Park and the serenity of the outlying islands, made all the more attractive by a public transport system as wide ranging and efficient as it is affordable.

Once you've sampled Hong Kong's heritage at a dragon boat race or one of the region's celebrated Chinese festivals, you can enjoy a taste of its renowned hedonism. Hong Kongers are a cosmopolitan bunch, as you'll soon discover at any number of authentic dim sum joints and slick lounge bars. This book will help you find the best among them.

The following pages have all the information you'll need for planning your trip as well as advice on the basics that will make life easier when you arrive. A good place so start your planning is the Hong Kong Checklist on p.6. These are things you really shouldn't miss. You'll also find some suggested itineraries for different moods and budgets.

In the Exploring chapter we've divided Hong Kong by its main areas and highlighted the best bits, such as museums and beaches, and a few places further out of town.

Sports & Spas discovers the many chances to get active in Hong Kong, whether on the golf course or climbing wall, as well as where to be pampered.

And Shopping is a detailed guide to the best boutiques, malls and markets, of which Hong Kong is rightly proud. Going Out again divides Hong Kong, but this time with eating, drinking and other merriment in mind.
The Profile chapter at the back runs through the sometimes complex history and culture which makes Hong Kong what it is today.

ⓘ Mapping HK

The Map section, which starts on p.284, includes vector maps of the entire region. Each chapter has colour coded references so that you can find the exact location of each restaurant, museum, beach and visitor attraction. See the inside back cover for a handy MTR (metro) map.

Hong Kong Checklist

01 See the Big Buddha

Lantau Island's major cultural attraction sits atop a hill beside the Po Lin Monastery. Climb the steps to appreciate this magnificent statue up close, then visit the exhibition gallery underneath and round off with a vegetarian lunch at the monastery. See p.81.

02 Visit the Peak at Night

Hong Kong is at its most spectacular when seen from above. Take the Peak Tram (p.70) to the top and marvel at the glittering panorama of city and harbour. The picture windows at Cafe Deco (p.259) allow you to eat while enjoying the view.

03 Dragon Boat Racing

Dragon boat races take place in bays and harbours all over Hong Kong, usually in June. Admire the elaborately carved and dressed dragon boats and enjoy the drum-thumping excitement of the final push to the finishing line. See p.144.

04 The Symphony of Lights

The waterfront at Tsim Sha Tsui is the best spot to enjoy the multimedia light show which takes place each night at 20:00. More than 30 buildings on both sides of the harbour are lit by laser beams during the spectacle. See p.108.

05 Shop Like a Local

Air-conditioned shopping malls spring up like weeds in Hong Kong but the street markets (p.176) still survive. Whether you're on the lookout for souvenirs, jade, flowers, clothing, collectibles, electronics or art, you're sure to find a willing vendor.

06 History and Culture

Hong Kong's diverting museums cover everything from history, railways, medicine and traditional heritage to coastal defence, science and art. They make a good fallback option in case of rainy weather, but are well worth visiting in their own right. P.64.

07 Have a Big Night Out

Nightlife is part and parcel of Hong Kong's identity. Whether you choose Lan Kwai Fong, SoHo, Wan Chai, Tsim Sha Tsui or Causeway Bay, there's a huge selection of venues where you can happily party until the sun comes up. See p.194.

08 See the Harbour

Taking a harbour tour (p.130) gives a great perspective of Hong Kong's greatest natural asset. It's best at dusk, when the cityscape starts to light up with neon on both sides of the water. Alternatively, a trip aboard the Star Ferry (p.46) is a fun and memorable experience.

09 Hop on a Tram

See the city from the top deck of a rattling, clanking old 'ding ding' (as Hongkongers call them). The ride is a bargain at just $2. Trams run frequently, so if the first one is too crowded, just wait for the next to ensure you get that all-important front seat upstairs. See p.51.

10 Step Inside a Temple

Chinese religion is a complicated affair: Buddhism, Taoism, Confucianism, animism and ancestor worship all play a jade-bangled hand in it. Find out what goes on by paying a visit to one of Hong Kong's many places of worship. See p.64.

Best of Hong Kong

For Big Spenders…

Hong Kong is teeming with upmarket shopping districts, designer boutiques and fine dining restaurants, all of which compare favourably with London and New York. No longer the haven of cheap electronic goods, HK is now a hunting ground for label conscious fashionistas. Start your spree at The Landmark (p.166), a luxury mall awash with flagship designer stores, including Harvey Nichols (p.170) and Christian Dior, then head to Lane Crawford (p.172) and Prince's Building (p.168) for cutting edge fashion and chic accessories. Compare credit bills over late lunch at one of Hong Kong's understated (but not underpriced) eateries (p.188) before a blow out at the races (p.146). Happy Valley and Sha Tin are the homes of horse racing in Hong Kong and provide a perfect full stop to a day's frittering.

For Outdoor Types…

Whether you prefer blister-inducing hikes or lazy days on the beach, Hong Kong has an abundance of beautiful open spaces. Repulse Bay (p.98) and South Bay are two of the best urban spots to unwind, while Lo So Shing Beach (p.87) and Shek O Beach (p.99) are quaint and surprisingly quiet. And there are plenty other beaches and parks besides (p.64). Walkers who want to explore beyond the city skyscrapers will find numerous trails and treks. More than 40% of Hong Kong's territory is protected by country parks and this is where you'll find some of the region's most dramatic and impressive scenery, not to mention the MacLehose Trail, a huge 100km walk across the New Territories.

For Socialites…

If you've come to Hong Kong to do nothing but drink until the wee hours you won't be disappointed. Head to any of the city's nightlife hotspots (p.188) after dark and you'll find restaurants and bars bursting with punters bedding in for the night. Make your way to Knutsford Terrace in Tsim Sha Tsui (p.242) for a laidback meal with friends – Balalaika (p.243) and Tutto Bene (p.248) are highly recommended. Lan Kwai Fong offers boisterous boozing at La Dolce Vita (p.221) and Al's Diner (p.217), while the infamous Wan Chai offers, well, anything, including close-to-the-bone Joe Banana's (p.257) and Klong (p.256). A word of warning: bars charge big prices for drinks, so be prepared to pay dearly for that hangover.

For Culture Junkies…

From Big Buddhas to budding thespians, Hong Kong has a rich and complex cultural landscape. Its architecture, sites of religious significance and burgeoning art scene draw on both western and eastern influences. And it's easy to mix and match them in a single day. Visit a Chinese temple in the morning (p.64), the colonial Museum of Tea Ware (p.70) early afternoon and the Fringe Club (p.68) for afters. Finish off with a true taste of Hong Kong with dim sum washed down with Chinese tea (p.188).

Visiting Hong Kong

Thanks to an ultra modern airport and the ingenious Octopus Card, arriving in – and travelling around – Hong Kong is largely hassle-free.

Getting There

Hong Kong actively encourages tourism, so for most visitors, arrival is pleasingly straightforward. Hong Kong International Airport is regularly ranked as one of the world's best – and busiest – airports. Yet there are few long queues, especially once you're past your initial baggage check-in. Immigration and security checks run smoothly, even at peak hours. Baggage for arrivals often appears on carousels 10 or 15 minutes after your plane lands, and ground transport into the city is plentiful and well-organised. The airport's atmosphere is light and pleasant. Although the choice of restaurants and shopping is hardly inspired, it is fairly wide-ranging. There are duty-free shops at arrivals and departures.

Once you're out into the arrivals area, you'll find all the services and transport you'll need admirably organised and laid out right in front of you. Money changing and ATMs, tourist and hotel information, transport options and tickets – it's all there, and all easy to use. Staff at airport service counters will speak English, and generally try quite hard to help visitors. You can find a map of the airport's arrival hall facilities at www.hongkongairport.com.

Airlines

Air Canada	2329 0973	www.aircanada.ca
Air China	2216 1088	www.airchina.com.cn
Air France	2180 2180	www.airfrance.com
Air India	2216 1088	www.airindia.com
Air New Zealand	2862 8988	www.airnewzealand.com.hk
Air Philippines	2216 1088	www.airphils.com
American Airlines	2826 9102	www.aa.com
British Airways	2216 1088	www.ba.com
Cathay Pacific	2747 1888	www.cathaypacific.com
China Airlines	2769 8391	www.china-airlines.com
Dragonair	2180 2180	www.dragonair.com
Emirates	2216 1088	www.emirates.com
HongKong Express	3151 1800	www.hongkongexpress.com
Japan Airlines	2847 4567	www.jal.co.jp
KLM Royal Dutch Airlines	2180 2180	www.klm.com.hk
Korean Air	2769 7511	www.koreanair.com
Lufthansa	2868 2313	www.lufthansa.com
Philippine Airlines	2301 9300	www.pal.com.ph
Qantas	28229 000	www.qantas.com.au
Qatar Airways	2769 6032	www.qatarairways.com
Royal Brunei Airlines	2869 8608	www.bruneiair.com
Singapore Airlines	2520 2233	www.singaporeair.com.hk
South African Airways	2877 3277	www.saa.co.za
Thai Airways	2876 6888	www.thaiair.com
United Airlines	2122 8256	www.unitedairlines.com.hk
Virgin Atlantic	2532 6060	www.virgin-atlantic.com

Essentials

Visiting Hong Kong

From the Airport

An extremely fast train, the Airport Express, runs from Hong Kong International Airport to stations in Kowloon and Central on Hong Kong island. Travel time to the city is just over 20 minutes. The platform for boarding the Airport Express is located in the arrivals area of HKIA, and with ticket machines and counters scattered all around the airport, it's very convenient if you're headed into the heart of the city. The website www.mtr.com.hk has more information, and enables you to book tickets in advance.

If your destination lies in other Hong Kong districts, your best bet for cheap transport may be the bus. As you exit the Arrivals hall at the airport you'll see desks operated by shuttle bus companies. They run regular services that call at all the major hotels in Kowloon and on the Island. Alternatively, you could opt for one of the regular, scheduled bus services that call at the airport. Several lines run into the city, covering most of the urban areas and new towns, with stops near many hotels. Taxis are also readily available at HKIA; a ride into the city will cost between $250 and $300.

Details of all of these travel options can be found on the airport's website, www.hongkongairport.com.

Frequent Flyer?

Passengers who have visited Hong Kong three times or more in the preceding 12 months can apply for a Frequent Visitor Card, which allows them to use the Frequent Visitor Channel upon arrival at the airport. The website www.hongkongairport.com has more details.

Visas & Customs

Travellers from most western and Asian countries are granted a visa-free stay on arrival. The length of stay varies from country to country, with UK citizens getting the best deal at 180 days and citizens of most other western countries (including Australia, New Zealand and the United States) getting 90 days. Citizens of some Eastern European, Asian and Middle Eastern countries get 30 or 14 days. The nationals of a number of former Soviet republics and some Asian and African countries require pre-approved visas to enter Hong Kong, so check your country's status carefully before booking tickets. You can find a full list of current tourist visa requirements at the Hong Kong Immigration Department's website www.immd.gov.hk/ehtml/hkvisas_4.htm. If you have to apply for a Hong Kong tourist visa, the procedure is explained at www.immd.gov.hk/ehtml/topical_11.htm.

Ironically, citizens of mainland China have a far more difficult time gaining access to Hong Kong, although restrictions have

The Octopus Card

One of the best features of Hong Kong's public transport system is that all modes of transport – except taxis – can be paid for using the same stored-value card system, called the Octopus. Getting an Octopus Card is almost mandatory for Hong Kong residents, and may well be worthwhile if you're visiting for more than a couple of days. They can also be used in convenience stores, supermarkets and some fast-food restaurants.

eased in recent years. Their visa arrangements are handled completely separately from citizens of other countries.

Clearing customs at Hong Kong airport, ferry terminals, and land border stations usually constitutes a simple wave-through, although you may be pulled aside and asked where you've come from, and subsequently have your luggage searched. The usual items – firearms, drugs, fireworks and endangered animals – are prohibited, but note that there are no restrictions on bringing in currencies and perfumes, and that carrying in food items is generally not a problem. You can find the full rundown at the Hong Kong Customs website, www.customs.gov.hk. The allowances for bringing alcohol and tobacco into Hong Kong are considered to be pretty low when compared to some other countries around the world, and were reduced further in April 2007. You are now allowed one litre of 'alcoholic liquor' and 60 cigarettes or 15 cigars.

People with Disabilities

Getting around Hong Kong in a wheelchair is a challenge. Crowded pavements, uneven surfaces, and the fact that crossing a road often means a subway or footbridge are some of the difficulties you will face. The recommended approach is to use a manual wheelchair and take a strong friend to help you up and down, rather than using an electric wheelchair.

There have been improvements, however, with new buildings such as the airport well designed for wheelchair access, and larger hotels also promoting wheelchair-friendly facilities. All MTR stations are officially 'accessible' but this can vary from simply taking a public lift, to asssitance from a member of staff. Many buses now have low floors to enable wheelchair access, but should be avoided at rush hour when there are simply too many people boarding. Finally, taxis are a good choice as the wheelchair is carried free-of-charge and they can take you closer to your destination.

Visitor Information

The Hong Kong Tourism Board (HKTB) offers reliable help and information to visitors. It can answer questions about what to see, where to buy specific items, and how to get places. It also publishes a variety of publications including event listings, and organises self-guided walking tours.

You can visit the HKTB offices on Hong Kong island in the Causeway Bay MTR station (near exit F), or in Kowloon at the Star Ferry concourse, Tsim Sha Tsui. Both are open daily between 08:00 and 20:00. You can also call its multi-lingual hotline (2508 1234), which is available between 09:00 and 18:00 daily, or visit the website at www. discoverhongkong.com.

Anyone for Tai Chi?

Visitors to Hong Kong can enjoy a free tai chi class, courtesy of the Hong Kong Tourism Board. Classes takes place on Monday, Wednesday, Thursday and Friday mornings at 08:00 near the Museum of Art in Tsim Sha Tsui, or Saturday at 09:00 at the Peak Tower. See www.discoverhongkong. com or call 2508 1234 for more details.

View from The Peak

Climate

Although Hong Kong lies in the tropics, its climate is seasonal. These seasons break down differently, however, from those in Europe or North America:

Winter comprises January and February. A typical winter's day is cool – in the teens – with a light jacket needed. Most years see a couple of surges of cold air that drop temperatures below 10°C for a few days. When it does get cold though, it's really cold – Hong Kong buildings are not heated, so heavier jackets and sweaters are needed.

In spring (March to May), temperatures are mild – usually around the low to mid 20s – but it's frequently cloudy, foggy and humid. The rainy season really gets going in May.

Summer (June to September) is hot and very wet – it can rain off-and-on for days on end. There are sunny days, too, but wilting humidity is a constant. Daytime highs are typically in the low 30s, and night time temperatures drop only into the high 20s.

Autumn (October to December) is lovely, with clear days and lower humidity. Temperatures gradually drop from shirt-sleeve warmth in October to the crisp high teens in December.

Typhoons can strike Hong Kong anytime between April and November. Hong Kong's concrete and steel buildings stand up well to typhoons, but the city shuts down when conditions seriously deteriorate and a 'number 8' signal or higher is declared in local media.

There are also rainstorm warnings issued when rainfall is so heavy it impedes transport, but these usually don't last long enough to have much effect on day-to-day activities.

Crime & Safety

Hong Kong is a safe place, with comparatively low crime rates, though you should be aware that pickpockets are known to operate in tourist areas. Simple common-sense steps will minimise the chance of any problems:

- Leave as many valuables as possible in your hotel safe, or better still, leave them at home.
- Keep bags closed, and valuable items such as wallets and mobile phones out of sight.
- Keep wallets and bags in front of your body where you can see and feel them.
- Don't leave bags hanging on the back of your seat in restaurants or bars.

Police

The local police wear blue uniforms, and are armed with revolvers. Hong Kong has one of the highest police-to-population ratios in the world, so you'll often see them patrolling on foot. The police on the street are generally approachable if you need simple help with directions, although their standard of English varies considerably. If you are the victim of a crime, you'll need to file a report at the local police station, which you can find by calling the hotline (2527 7177). In an emergency, dial 999.

Dos & Don'ts

Note that in an effort to make Hong Kong a cleaner place, there are on-the-spot fines of $1,500 for people caught spitting or littering. Otherwise, the local laws are based on the

British judicial system, so as long as you follow normal good behaviour, you shouldn't find yourself in trouble.

Electricity

The electrical system in Hong Kong follows the UK standard (220 volts, 50Hz), and also uses the UK-style three-pin plugs. Plug adaptors are available in shops, and should be provided by your hotel. Hong Kong's power supply is very reliable, and power cuts are extremely rare.

Three to Know

A few easy phrases that will get a good response during your visit are:
'Joe san', meaning 'good morning'; a common greeting before lunch.
'Mm goi', meaning 'thank you', for small actions, e.g. someone gives you change, or moves something out of your way.
'Doh jeh', also meaning 'thank you', but used when someone has given you a gift, or has really gone out of their way to help you.

Language

The official languages of Hong Kong are Chinese and English, with spoken announcements typically repeated in both the Cantonese and Putonghua dialects of Chinese. In business, English is widely understood, though meetings will often be conducted in a mix of Chinese and English. Shops and restaurants in the business district and tourist areas will usually have English-speaking staff available, and English menus are available in most

Basic Cantonese

General

Good morning	joe san
My name is...	ngoh giu...
Please	mm goi
Thank you	mm goi / doh jeh
You're welcome	m saai haak hei
How are you?	nei hou maa?
Very good; very well	hou hou
Excuse me; sorry	m hou yi si
Goodbye	joi gin

Questions

How much?	gei do cheen ?
Where?	bin dou?
When?	gei si?
Which? Who?	bin go?
Why?	dim gaai?
What?	sam mo?

Taxi / Car Related

Stop	ting
Right	yau
Left	jaw
Go straight ahead	jik hoi
Go slowly	maan maan
Intersection, turning	gaai hau

Road	lou
Street	gaai
Roundabout	wui syun chiu
Traffic light	hung luk dang
Close to something	gan jue
Petrol station	yau jaam
Beach	saa taan
Airport	gei cheung
Hotel	jau dim
Bank	ngan hong
Restaurant	chaan teng

Numbers

Zero	ling
One	yat
Two	yee
Three	saam
Four	sei
Five	ng
Six	luk
Seven	chat
Eight	baat
Nine	gau
Ten	sup
Hundred	baak
Thousand	cheen

Essentials

Local Knowledge

restaurants. If you venture out to the residential areas, or out of the city altogether, you may have more trouble finding an English speaker. If you are worried about finding your way, it's worth getting the address and directions written out in Chinese.

For the words and phrases in the table on the previous page we've given a phonetic equivalent of the Cantonese, although it has to be said that you're not likely to be understood if you try to pronounce them. Cantonese is a tonal language and has sounds that are not commonly used in western languages.

You'll notice there are no entries for yes and no, as in Cantonese you ask and answer questions differently from English. The words 'yes' and 'no' are widely understood however, so just use those with a nod or shake of the head as appropriate.

Lost/Stolen Property

If you lose property, or it is stolen, you'll need to make a report to the local police station as quickly as possible. Ask your hotel or call the hotline (2527 7177) to find the location of the nearest station.

If you think you left something in a taxi, call the taxi hotline (187 2920) and they will broadcast details to all drivers. For public transport, call the company's hotline for help (see below). Remember also to cancel any missing credit cards by calling the relevant company: American Express (2811 6122), Mastercard (800 966 677), or Visa (800 900 782). You'll also need to contact your country's consulate if you have lost your passport.

You should also check your travel insurance policy to see how the loss should be reported.

Lost/Stolen Property Hotlines	
Citybus Ltd	2873 0818
Hong Kong Tramways Ltd	2548 7102
Kowloon-Canton Railway Corporation (KCR)	2929 3399
Kowloon Motor Bus Co (1933) Ltd	2745 4466
Mass Transit Railway (MTR) Corporation	2881 8888
New Lantau Bus Co (1973) Ltd	2984 9848
New World First Bus Services Ltd	2136 8888
New World First Ferry Services Ltd	2131 8181
Peak Tramways Co Ltd	2522 0922
The 'Star' Ferry Co Ltd	2367 7065

Money

Hong Kong's currency is the dollar, divided into 100 cents. Coins are available in 10c, 20c, 50c, $1, $2, $5, and $10 denominations. Notes available are the $10, $20, $50, $100, $500 and $1,000.

You can expect to see several different designs of each note during your visit, as three of the local banks (HSBC, Standard Chartered, and Bank of China) issue their own notes. Although their designs differ, they all follow the same colour scheme, except new $10 notes are purple and $50 notes green, but there are still older green $10 notes and purple $50 notes in circulation. Hotels and large shops in the tourist areas will often accept payment in other currencies, especially US$ and Chinese renminbi. Outside those areas, expect to use Hong Kong dollars.

If you are visiting from the US, currency translation is straightforward as the HK$ has been pegged to the US$ since 1983, at the rate of HK$7.8 for every US$1.

Credit cards are widely accepted for payment in Hong Kong, especially Visa and Mastercard. In smaller shops, or for smaller purchases (say less than $200), you may find that only cash is accepted. When paying with your card try to

Make a Copy

Before travelling to Hong Kong, make copies of your essential documents and keep them in a safe place – either back home or in your hotel safe once you arrive. They will come in very handy if you're unfortunate enough to lose the originals.

keep it in sight at all times to avoid your card being skimmed and cloned.

Most banks have their head office in Central district on Hong Kong island, but you'll find sub-branches distributed throughout the built-up areas of Hong Kong. Banks are open from 09:00 to 16:30 Monday to Friday, and 09:00 to 12:30 on Saturdays. Note that smaller branches don't offer currency exchange services.

You won't have to walk far to find an ATM. Bank branches have ATMs outside, every MTR station has them, and shopping malls usually have several too. You should not have any problem using your home bank's debit or credit card here, as local ATMs support the two global ATM networks, Cirrus and PLUS.

When you need to change currency, hotels typically offer the least competitive rates, taking around 7% of your money for the privilege. Banks are a safer bet, and charge between 2 and 3%, with good money exchanges charging 1 to 2%. You can get better rates than these on popular currencies such as the US$, while relatively rare currencies will get you a worse rate. Money exchanges are easy to find – just look for their brightly lit 'Change' signs; they're typically open between 09:30 and 19:30.

However, beware the changers on main streets in the heart of the tourist areas (for example along Ashley Road in Tsim Sha Tsui), who can charge more than15%. If this all sounds like too much trouble, using an ATM to withdraw money from your home bank account is fast, available every hour of the day, and typically costs you between 2 and 3%.

Postal Services

Hong Kong has an efficient postal service, for both local and overseas mail. For example, it costs $3 to send a postcard by airmail to Australia, the UK or US, and it will arrive in seven days or less. You can buy stamps at local post offices, or from the 7-Eleven and Circle-K chains of convenience stores. Stamps are also available from vending machines located in, or just outside, post offices. Post boxes are painted green.

Tipping

Tipping is not universally expected in Hong Kong, but always appreciated. The actual amount to tip varies according to who you are dealing with:

- Taxis – the driver will usually just round the fare up to the nearest dollar; in any case, that's all you need to pay.
- Hotel washroom attendants – they appreciate a small tip, say $2.
- Ordinary restaurants – let's say you pay for a $400 meal with a $500 note. You're surprised to see that the change comes back as a $50 and two $20 notes, plus some coins, ie. a $5, two $2s, and a $1. It isn't that the cashier didn't have a $100 note. Instead, she's guiding you in making a tip – in this case you take the notes and the $5 coin, and leave the small coins. Even when paying by credit card, local practice is just to round up to give a tip in $5 to $20 range. You really don't need to calculate the tip as a percentage of the total bill.
- Bellhops – give them $10 to $20 depending on the number of bags they are carrying for you.

The Clocktower in Tsim Sha Tsui

- Salons – if you get a haircut, take a massage, or visit a beauty salon, a 5 to10% tip will be welcomed, and you'll get an extra smile on your next visit.
- Hotel restaurants, and other upmarket restaurants – a 10% service charge will be added to the bill automatically, but it won't go to the staff. An extra 5 to10% tip will be appreciated if you had good service – leave it as cash if you are paying by credit card, so that it goes to the waiters.

Telephone & Internet

Mobile phones in Hong Kong work on a GSM 900 system (Global System for Mobile Telephones) or other networks such as PCS 1800 and CDMA. There is a roaming agreement set up with most international networks. There are six mobile phone service providers in Hong Kong running 11 networks. Their retail shops can be easily found in the main shopping malls and streets. Visitors can buy a SIM card from as little as $48, which you can top up when credit is running low. If you're a frequent visitor you can re-register the SIM every six months to keep the same number. Arriving passengers can rent a mobile phone at the airport (2883 3938) – rentals start at about $35 per day with a refundable deposit of $500.

Internet access is available all over the region, with very good wireless coverage in most urban areas. Many coffee shops offer free internet use to their customers and there are hundreds of restaurants offering wireless broadband. For those without a laptop or pda try one of Pacific Coffee's many branches – most have two or three computers for customer use. For locations, see www.pacificcoffee.com. If you prefer healthy juices while you surf the net free of charge, try The Mix. Most of their stores are on Hong Kong Island, but you can also find them in Sha Tin and Hong Kong International Airport. Visit www.mix-world.com for locations.

Time & Opening Hours

Hong Kong is eight hours ahead of UCT (Universal Coordinated Time – formerly known as GMT). That means if it is 12:00 midday in Hong Kong it is 13:00 in Tokyo, 09:30 in Delhi, 04:00 in London, and 23:00 the previous day in New York. Hong Kong does not alter its clocks for daylight savings or summer time.

Should you need them for any reason, most government offices are open between 09:00 and 17:00, Monday to Friday, and with the recent scrapping of Saturday working, many are now open earlier in the morning and later at night. Some, however, do still open on Saturday mornings.

Shops are open seven days a week. Shops in the Central district typically open between 10:00 and 19:00, closing after the office workers leave for home. In popular shopping areas such as Tsim Sha Tsui or Causeway Bay, however, shops stay open till at least 20:00 or 21:00, and if you visit Mong Kok you'll find the streets are still busy and shops are open well past 22:00.

Opening times for restaurants and bars are generally unaffected by public holidays. The only possible exception is likely to be Chinese New Year.

Newspapers & Magazines

Hong Kong's main English-language local newspaper is the *South China Morning Post*, or SCMP, priced at $7 a copy. The SCMP covers all areas you'd expect in a modern daily, with particular coverage of Hong Kong and China news. The other local English daily is *The Standard* ($6), which is more business focussed. It's worth picking up *HK Magazine* for weekly listings and restaurant reviews.

There are newspaper stands on every busy pavement, and 7-Eleven and Circle K convenience stores also sell papers. Some newsstands also carry a selection of overseas newspapers and magazines, as do the Bookazine and Page One stores. The overseas newspapers will typically be at least two days old though. Finally, if you just like browsing (or if you're a cheapskate), visit the fifth floor of the Hong Kong Central Library in Causeway Bay (map p.295 F-4). You don't need a library card; just walk in and take your pick from current issues of more than 300 newspapers and 4,000 periodicals.

TV & Radio

There are two domestic, free terrestrial television channels in English: ATV World (Asia Television) and TVB (Television Broadcast) Pearl, both offering a mix of entertainment and current affairs programmes, mainly from the US and the UK. All major hotels have cable or satellite TV, offering the usual array of international channels.

Radio Television Hong Kong (RTHK) broadcasts a number of radio channels in both English and Chinese.

Books

James Clavell's novels (*Tai Pan* and *Noble House*) are set in Hong Kong. They are definitely fiction, but you'll also pick up a feel for life in Hong Kong, and its culture and customs. If you prefer non-fiction, Frank Walsh's *A History of Hong Kong* covers exactly what its title suggests, while Martin Booth's *Memoir Gweilo: Memories of a Hong Kong Childhood* is a charming tale of life in Hong Kong as a child in the 1950s.

Websites & Blogs

Below are some useful websites. You can also check out some of the local blogs for a more informal take on Hong Kong life; an internet search for 'Hong Kong blog' will quickly take you to popular sites. Recommended are www.batgung.com and www.ordinarygweilo.com.

Websites	
www.asia-city.com	What's on & restaurant reviews
www.centamap.com	HK maps, with search function
www.cityline.com.hk	Cinema listings & online booking
www.discoverhongkong.com	Hong Kong Tourism Board
www.geoexpat.com	Forums, classifieds, etc
www.hkoutdoors.com	Hong Kong's countryside
www.gov.hk	Government portal
www.scmp.com	Local newspaper (subscription)
www.thestandard.com.hk	Local newspaper
www.yp.com.hk	Hong Kong Yellow Pages

Whatever time of year, there's a wealth of historic and culturally significant events for visitors to enjoy.

Hong Kong has 17 public holidays per year, which fall into three main groups. First come the Christian holidays of Christmas and Easter. Then there's a patriotic group including Labour Day, National Day, and the snappily titled 'Hong Kong Special Administrative Region Establishment Day'. Finally, the bulk are traditional Chinese cultural holidays such as Lunar New Year and the Ching Ming festival, which have been celebrated in Chinese communities for hundreds if not thousands of years. These holidays are based on a traditional lunar calendar, so they move around year by year.
Some other points to think about:

· If a public holiday falls on a Sunday, the following Monday is given as the holiday instead.
· The land borders to China are very busy around public holidays, and are best avoided.
· China has three 'Golden Week' national holidays per year, corresponding to the Hong Kong public holidays for the Lunar New Year, Labour Day, and National Day. During these weeks, basically all of China is on holiday at the same time.
· Lunar New Year (more commonly known as Chinese New Year or just CNY) is the most important holiday in the Chinese calendar. It is the one time of year that most of Hong Kong's shops and businesses close, with many people travelling home to spend the time with their families.

Two holidays you should make the effort to attend are the Tuen Ng Festival (more commonly known as the 'Dragon Boat Festival'), and the Mid-Autumn Festival. See p.42 for more details.

See p.42 for more details.

Public Holidays	2007	2008
The first day of January	01-Jan	01-Jan
The day preceding Lunar New Year's Day	17-Feb	–
Lunar New Year's Day	–	07-Feb
The second day of the Lunar New Year	19-Feb	08-Feb
The third day of the Lunar New Year	20-Feb	09-Feb
Ching Ming Festival	05-Apr	04-Apr
Good Friday	06-Apr	21-Mar
The day following Good Friday	07-Apr	22-Mar
Easter Monday	09-Apr	24-Mar
Labour Day	01-May	01-May
The Buddha's Birthday	24-May	12-May
Tuen Ng Festival	19-Jun	–
The day following Tuen Ng Festival	–	09-Jun
Hong Kong SAR Establishment Day	–	01-Jul
The day following Hong Kong SAR Establishment Day	02-Jul	–
The day following Chinese Mid-Autumn Festival	26-Sep	15-Sep
National Day	01-Oct	01-Oct
Chung Yeung Festival	19-Oct	07-Oct
Christmas Day	25-Dec	25-Dec
The first weekday after Christmas Day	26-Dec	26-Dec

Annual Events

Chinese (Lunar) New Year
February (Lunar date)
This is the biggest and most famous festival in the Chinese calendar, when everyone makes the effort to spend time at home with their families and friends. It's the one time of the year when Hong Kong feels quiet, with many shops and businesses closed. Major events held over the three-day holiday include a huge fireworks display over the harbour, and a street parade of floats, performers and marching bands from around the world.

Cheung Chau Bun Festival
May (Lunar date)
Cheung Chau
www.cheungchau.org
One of the more unusual events in Hong Kong, this week-long festival on Cheung Chau Island culminates in a parade of costumed children on stilts, and a mad race to the top of bun-clad bamboo towers. The higher the bun, the greater the glory.

Cricket Sixes
November
Kowloon Cricket Club
www.hksixes.com
This is your best chance to see international cricket in East Asia, with all the leading cricketing nations represented. The weekend-long Sixes is cricket's answer to the Rugby Sevens. As with the Sevens, the Sixes follows a format that encourages a faster, more entertaining game, and attracts a wider audience than the usual cricket buffs.

Dragon Boat Festival

June (Lunar calendar date)

Various Locations   www.discoverhongkong.com

The official name is the 'Tuen Ng Festival', but you'll remember it as the dragon boat festival. Head to the seafront to see teams of around 20 sitting in slender dragon boats, paddling furiously to the beat of their drummers. Local races are held near fishing villages such as Aberdeen and Stanley, with the international races usually held a week or so later in Sha Tin.

Hong Kong Arts Festival

February/March

Various Locations

Get a dose of culture at Hong Kong's main arts event. With a mix of overseas and local artists, and a variety of music, theatre, dance, popular entertainment and film programmes, you're sure to find something that catches your fancy.

Hong Kong International Film Festival   March/April

Various Locations   www.hkiff.org.hk

Leave reality behind and indulge in over two weeks of cinema. Hollywood and indie, local and international, old and new. With several hundred films to choose from, there is a bit of everything. One note of warning – popular films are often sold out, so book early.

Hong Kong Marathon

February

Races start from Tsim Sha Tsui   www.hkmarathon.com

The highlight for runners is the chance to run across the Tsing Ma suspension bridge, normally the roadway from the city to the airport. If running 26 miles in Hong Kong's polluted air seems like too much, there are also half marathon and 10K races held the same day.

Hong Kong Sevens
Hong Kong Stadium

March
www.hksevens.com

The Sevens offers a weekend of fast-paced, exciting rugby, and attracts fans from around the world. Teams from 24 nations compete, including all the world's rugby majors. For many, the close of play each day marks the start of a long night – head to Wan Chai and Lan Kwai Fong to join the party.

Lan Kwai Fong Julyfest
Lan Kwai Fong

July
www.lankwaifong.com

You probably don't need an excuse to visit Lan Kwai Fong, Hong Kong's bar & club centre. Still, on this day things go that bit further, with stalls on the street serving food and drinks from lunchtime onwards. There is a variety of performances and competitions to keep you busy, with the party carrying on late into the night.

Mid-Autumn Festival
Various Locations

October (Lunar calendar date)

This public holiday is the strangely named 'The day following Chinese Mid-Autumn Festival'. The reason is that on the evening of the actual festival children head to open spaces carrying lanterns, hoping to see the full moon. It's a late night, so the following day is a public holiday. All the illuminated lanterns make for a pretty sight, so get out for a walk in a park that evening – Victoria Park and the Peak are good bets.

Getting Around

It may seem intimidating at first, but Hong Kong's transport network is slick, safe and super efficient.

Boat

Hong Kong's most famous transport link is the venerable Star Ferry, which sloshes back and forth between Hong Kong island and Kowloon in about 10 minutes. You are sure to take the Star Ferry at least once during your visit.

Less picturesque, but much faster, ferries play a big part in Hong Kong's overall transport network, with multiple routes connecting the inhabited outlying islands, and a few spots in the New Territories, with the city. Most ferries these days are fast ones, with fully enclosed, air-conditioned cabins, but some routes still mix in older slow ferries with open decks that can be very pleasant for seeing a different face of Hong Kong. The main ferry companies are New World First Ferry Services (www.nwff.com.hk), Hong Kong & Kowloon Ferry Ltd (www.hkkf.com.hk) and Discovery Bay Transportation Services (www.hkri.com). Fast ferry services to Macau and Shenzhen are operated by New World First Ferry and TurboJet (www.turbojet.com.hk).

Bus

Many visitors (and residents) find Hong Kong's complex bus networks a bit intimidating and avoid using them. This is a mistake, because large – and interesting – parts of the region are not accessible from the MTR and other trains. Bus frequency is generally good. You rarely wait longer than 15 minutes, and much shorter waits are the norm. The buses are quite comfortable. Most are air-conditioned double-deckers. The websites of the three major bus companies provide excellent route information, including photos of each individual bus stop: Citybus (www.citybus.com.hk), Kowloon Motor Bus (www.kmb.com.hk), and New World First Bus (www.nwfb.com.hk).

Car

Tourists are not advised to hire a car in Hong Kong. Roads are crowded and complex, parking is expensive, and public transport and taxis are all you'll need to see the city and its sights. Renting cars in the region is also very expensive.

If you decide you really must rent a car, Hertz and Avis will be happy to take your money. You have few other choices. There are small local car rental agencies aplenty, but they're generally more interested in arranging tours and drivers. One you could try is Jubilee International (2530 0530). Base rental prices range from $500 to $700 per day for a compact car to $1,000 per day or more for a larger car.

Minibuses

There are two types: the cream-and-green ones follow set routes with more or less official 'stops', much like ordinary buses. The cream-and-red ones have more freedom; they generally follow a point-to-point route, but they can pick up and drop off passengers wherever they like, much as a taxi would.

Weekly prices start at $2,500 for a compact, and $4,000 or more for a bigger model.

Taxi

Hong Kong is well-served by taxis. They're relatively cheap – the starting price in urban-area taxis is $15 – and even a very long trip, for example, from the airport into town, costs about $300. Unless it's raining or rush hour, taxis are easy to find.

All Hong Kong taxis are metered, and although occasional scams are reported, Hong Kong cabbies are mostly reliable.

Red-and-grey urban taxis can go anywhere in Hong Kong. There are also separate sets of taxis restricted to the New Territories (green) and Lantau Island (blue).

One quirk to keep in mind is that urban drivers further divide themselves according to the side of the harbour they prefer to work on; that is, there are 'Hong Kong side', and 'Kowloon side' taxis. When you do take a cross-harbour taxi ride, remember that you will have to pay double the tunnel fee: once to cross with you in the taxi, and once to get the driver back over to 'his side'. You can get by with paying a single tunnel fee by tracking down one of the special taxi ranks exclusively devoted to drivers looking to get back across the harbour.

Car Rental Agencies		
Avis	2890 6988	www.avis.com
Hertz Rent A Car	2525 1313	www.hertz.com
Jubilee International	2530 0530	www.jubilee.com.hk

Hong Kong taxis

Most taxi drivers will be able to understand your directions in English – if your destination is well-known, that is. But if it's not, it's best to get your destination written out for you in Chinese. Your hotel concierge will be happy to do this.

Train

The mostly underground Mass Transit Railway (MTR) and above-ground Kowloon-Canton Railway (KCR) comprise the most visitor-friendly transport network in Hong Kong.

The MTR comprises five main lines, plus one short line dedicated to serving Hong Kong Disneyland. Most lines run underground, but in places the MTR comes hurtling out of hillsides and you're suddenly on elevated platforms running right through the city. Most of the core urban areas, on both Hong Kong island and Kowloon, are within 10 minutes' walk of an MTR station. The MTR has built up a well-deserved reputation as one of the world's best public transport systems. Trains are spotless, bright and well air conditioned, and run at minute-to-minute frequency at peak hours. MTR stations are also clean and safe. The KCR, comprising three main lines plus ancillary light rail and

Parking

Parking in Hong Kong is rarely free, and most areas of the city have no street-level parking whatsoever. Most carparks are situated in the lower levels of residential buildings and shopping malls. Hourly costs are high, ranging from $8 to 10 per hour in outlying areas, up to $30 per hour or more in the heart of the city.

bus services, is primarily a suburban system, serving 'new towns' such as Sha Tin, Tai Po and Ma On Shan.

The major drawback of both Hong Kong's train systems can be summed up in two words: rush hour. The morning congestion (08:00 to 09:30) is the worst, but trains also get very busy between 18:00 and 19:00.

Tram

Hong Kong's trams are still used daily by thousands of people moving along the north side of Hong Kong island. Trams are not fast, or particularly comfortable, but they have undeniable charm and a great view from the front of the upper deck. For short journeys they're sometimes quicker than bus or train, and certainly far cheaper.

Walking

In many areas, above and below ground walkways are provided for pedestrians. Tsim Sha Tsui, one of the city's busiest districts, is now honeycombed with bright, pleasant pedestrian tunnels. Still, in no matter what part of the city, you'll often find yourself standing at large intersections waiting to cross.

In many areas pavements get seriously congested, almost to the point of pedestrian gridlock, and in parts of Hong Kong island 'walking' means 'climbing steps'. Getting 'up the hill' on the island is greatly aided by an extensive escalator system that takes riders up from the CBD through trendy SoHo's restaurants and pubs, and on up to the residential Mid-Levels. Walking is safe virtually everywhere in the city.

Places to Stay

Hong Kong's hotels range from fancy, lavish affairs with harbour views to humble hostels in the countryside. Occupancy rates are high, so book well in advance.

Most of Hong Kong's hotels are grouped in the business and tourist areas around the harbour. In Kowloon, that means Tsim Sha Tsui and Tsim Sha Tsui East, while on the island it's the strip from Central through to Causeway Bay. Recent years have seen hotels popping up in more remote areas, and their rates can be cheaper, if you don't mind the extra travelling.

The Hong Kong Tourism Board claims that there is no need for any hotel star-rating system, as 'the laws of supply and demand have ensured that Hong Kong's hotels maintain the highest standards'. Dig a bit deeper and you'll find that internally the Tourism Board divides hotels into four categories – but don't make the results public.

Even within the same hotel you'll find a wide range of prices depending on the season, the size of the room, and the view. Ah, the view. If you are staying in one of the more exclusive hotels, it's worth paying the extra to get the harbour view – it's something you'll certainly remember from your trip. Make sure you get a room with a full harbour view though, as on lower floors you may just be getting a glimpse of the sea. If you have to walk into a hotel to find a room, the rack rate might come as a suprise so ask for the 'walk in' specials and you should get a better deal.

Conrad Hong Kong
www.conradhotels.com
2521 3838
The hotel is located above Pacific Place, and has good transport connections, so a short ride in a taxi or on the MTR can get you to most of the places you'll want to go. Many of the rooms have Peak views.

🚇 Admiralty, Map p.298 B-1

Four Seasons
www.fourseasons.com/hongkong
3196 8888
The Four Seasons has probably the best hotel location on the island. It's perfect for business, but a spa and two outdoor infinity pools overlooking the harbour make it a great place to relax as well.

🚇 Hong Kong, Map p.291 E-1

Grand Hyatt
www.hongkong.grand.hyatt.com
2584 7878
This hotel has an unusually large outdoor sports area, including an 80m pool, tennis courts and a golf driving range. You'll also find a range of top-quality restaurants, and the recently re-opened JJ's nightclub.

🚇 Wan Chai, Map p.293 E-3

Places to Stay

InterContinental Grand Stanford
www.hongkong.intercontinental.com
2721 5161
Located in Tsim Sha Tsui East, this hotel
has 578 rooms and suites, half of which
enjoy views over Victoria Harbour.
Facilities include a rooftop heated
swimming pool, and great dining options.
🚇 Tsim Sha Tsui, Map p.303 F-2

InterContinental Hong Kong
www.hongkong-ic.intercontinental.com
2721 1211
The InterContinental offers perfect views
across the harbour. Facilities include an
outdoor heated pool and the feng shui
inspired I-Spa, while diners can enjoy the
popular restaurant, SPOON.
🚇 Tsim Sha Tsui, Map p.303 D-4

Island Shangri-La
www.shangri-la.com
2877 3838
The Shangri-La has a reputation for
excellent service, whether you are staying
for business or pleasure. From the hotel
there's easy access to the Pacific Place
complex and nearby Hong Kong Park.
🚇 Admiralty, Map p.298 B-1

JW Marriott

www.marriott.com/hkgdt

2810 8366

With 577 rooms and 25 suites offering views of the harbour, city or mountains, this hotel focuses on the needs of the business traveller. Facilities include 15 meeting rooms, six dining outlets, and a health club. 🚇 Admiralty, Map p.298 C-1

Kowloon Shangri-La

www.shangri-la.com

2721 2111

Each of the 700 rooms and suites has either a king-sized bed or two double beds, and floor-to-ceiling windows, offering fine views. There are superb restaurants and bars, and top fitness facilities.

🚇 Tsim Sha Tsui, Map p.303 E-3

The Landmark Mandarin Oriental

www.mandarinoriental.com

2132 0188

If you like slick, modern hotels, then this is a good choice. There are flat panel TVs in each of the 113 rooms and suites, plus the ability to plug your iPod into the sound system. There is also an impressive two-floor spa. 🚇 Central, Map p.291 F-3

Langham Hotel

http://hongkong.langhamhotels.com

2375 1133

This hotel is within easy reach of the MTR station and TST's commercial and entertainment options, and has 495 rooms and suites, a rooftop swimming pool, a 24 hour gym with sauna, and six restaurants and a bar. Tsim Sha Tsui, Map p.302 B-3

Langham Place Hotel

http://hongkong.langhamhotels.com

3552 3388

Located in the heart of Kowloon, this hotel has 665 rooms, hotel-wide broadband, four restaurants, and five function rooms. The top three floors house the Chuan Spa, and there is a heated rooftop pool.

Mong Kok, Map p.306 B-2

Mandarin Oriental

www.mandarinoriental.com/hongkong

2522 0111

This hotel has 502 rooms and suites, all with either a harbour or city view. Leisure facilities include the Mandarin Spa, an indoor pool, and a fitness centre. Business visitors can take advantage of the of the 'IT butler'. Central, Map p.291 F-3

The Peninsula

www.peninsula.com

2920 2888

You'll want to visit The Peninsula even if you aren't staying here. High tea in the lobby, drinks at sunset in the Felix Bar, or excellent French cuisine at Gaddi's, are all waiting to tempt you to Hong Kong's best-known hotel. 📷 Tsim Sha Tsui, Map p.302 C-4

Ritz-Carlton, Hong Kong

www.ritzcarlton.com/hotels/hong_kong

2877 6666

Located in the heart of the business district and close to major shopping, entertainment and dining areas, the Ritz-Carlton has 216 rooms (with harbour or Peak views), six restaurants, and a hot tub on the roof. 📷 Central, Map p.292 A-3

Sheraton Hong Kong Hotel & Towers

www.starwoodhotels.com

2369 1111

The Sheraton offers easy access to the attractions of TST, and has a health club, spa, sauna, and massage facilities. There is also a business centre. There are 782 guest rooms and suites (many with a harbour view). 📷 Tsim Sha Tsui, Map p.303 D-3

Hotel Apartments

If you'll be staying for a month or more then serviced apartments are often a better choice than hotels. You can get similar facilities, including a pool, gym, etc, but in fully furnished accommodation that is more spacious and feels more like a home than a hotel room.

Check the latest prices for standard accommodation with Shama (www.shama.com) who have properties across town. For deluxe accommodation you can expect to pay at least $30,000 per month, and $100,000 for larger apartments.

Guest Houses

If you are looking for budget accommodation and don't mind basic facilities, a guest house is another option. Make sure it is licensed (the government has a list at www.hadla.gov.hk), and that it is a 'Tourist Guesthouse'. The alternative is 'Local People Guesthouses', which are aimed at the Chinese market.

Chungking Mansions in Tsim Sha Tsui (TST) was traditionally the focal point for budget accommodation, but it is an old and crowded building. You are better off staying elsewhere, as there is plenty of choice. See the table below for some suggestions.

Guest Houses

Chung Kiu Inn	2895 3304	www.chungkiuinn.com.hk
Wang Fat Hostel	2895 1015	www.wangfathostel.com.hk
Cosmic Guest House	2369 6669	www.cosmicguesthouse.com
Man Hing Lung Hotel	2311 8807	www.manhinglung-hotel.com

In Causeway Bay, expect to pay between $300 and $400 per night for a double room, while in Tsim Sha Tsui the rate is between $200 and $300 per night. Ask about discounts if you'll be staying a week or longer. Rooms have a small private toilet and shower, TV and air conditioning. That's about all the facilities you should expect, though you may be surprised to find that all four listed on p.58 offer WiFi wireless internet.

Hostels

Several organisations operate hostels in Hong Kong, including the Youth Hostels Association (YHA). Most of the YHA's hostels are located in the countryside, so they are of limited interest to short-term visitors. The exception is the Mount Davis hostel (2788 1638, www.yha.org.hk), located at the top of a hill at the western end of Hong Kong island. Great views, low-cost (dormitory beds from $80 a night), but it is also rather inconveniently located.

If location is important, the best bargain is the YMCA's 'The Salisbury', in Tsim Sha Tsui (2268 7888, www.ymcahk.org. hk). It offers modern accommodation in the heart of the tourist area, with a bed in a four-person dormitory costing just $230 a night.

i Backpacking?

Supermarkets are well stocked, and small local Chinese restaurants will fill you up for $30 or so. Check out happy-hour offers for drinks, or get a bottle or two of local beer with your meal. If you avoid taxis, public transport is inexpensive, and many attractions are free or inexpensive to visit.

Exploring

Exploring Hong Kong

From the bustling streets and the shimmering harbour to the picturesque mountains not so far away, Hong Kong is yours to explore.

If you are an explorer at heart – then Hong Kong will provide plenty for you to search out and discover. It's surprisingly rich in cultural and scenic gems. With a city so dense, a territory so mountainous and a coastline so indented, a modest 1000 sq km can provide an incredible number of attractions.

A number of stock labels are regularly applied to Hong Kong – Pearl of the Orient, City of Life, Asia's World City – but these do little to describe the great diversity which exists within this unique region on the coast of China. Hong Kong is a meeting point of cultures from all over Asia and beyond. Its heritage draws on influences from the imperial Chinese, the colonial British, and traders and adventurers of a hundred nationalities; and it is home to communities from all corners of the world. Food, architecture, religion, government and language all bear the imprints of a century and more of international exchange.

The glittering harbour is the centrepiece of a loud, crowded, sometimes overwhelming city, but it is compact, and escape to the mountains or islands is quick and easy. Hong Kong's public transport is cheap, frequent and goes almost everywhere. The areas not covered by MTR or KCR trains are generally saturated by bus routes, and you'll find that even the smallest village is served by a green minibus.

Where minibuses fail, then there is always the taxi, also relatively cheap and in good supply. Regular ferry services are supplemented by sampans and 'kaido' village ferries. An Octopus card is a useful tool for public transport, but as yet it is not accepted in taxis or red minibuses.

Besides transport, sightseeing is also very affordable. If no admission fee is mentioned for the following entries, you can assume there is none. Some municipal museums charge a token fee for entry, usually as little as $10 for adults, but even that is often waived on one day per week.

If time is short, then there is a range of guided tours aimed at people who want to see a lot in a few hours. See the Tours & Sightseeing section starting on p.126. If you need a change of pace, surroundings or culture, then it's easy to visit the border cities of China, or the former Portuguese enclave of Macau.

Each of Hong Kong's areas has its own character, sights and environment, whether rural or urban. Each area is described in detail in the following pages, allowing you to plan a daytrip. Use this chapter in conjunction with the maps that start on p.284.

As Hong Kong people say, jau la – let's go.

> ### Explore This Site
> **The website of the Leisure and Cultural Services Department (LCSD) is a good resource for people wishing to explore Hong Kong. The site features information on the region's parks, beaches and other leisure facilities, plus details of museums and heritage attractions. See www.lcsd.gov.hk.**

Heritage Sites

Museums & Art Galleries

Beaches & Parks

Sights and Attractions

Central & Mid-Levels

Don't be fooled by the forgettable name. This is the original heart of Hong Kong, home of big business, boisterous boozing and designer boutiques.

Officially known as Victoria until the name went out of fashion, the financial and administrative centre of Hong Kong now goes by the more prosaic name of Central. It's still the headquarters of government and big business, with local and international banks and hongs (trading houses) represented by ever-higher and shinier office towers.

Land has been reclaimed here ever since Hong Kong was first settled and, to the dismay of harbour activists, it's an ongoing process. Queen's Road Central roughly follows the route of the original shoreline.

Statue Square is the nearest thing Hong Kong has to an official city centre. It's worth standing here to take in some of the landmarks. With your back to the harbour, you face the striking headquarters of HSBC and, to its left, the angular Bank of China. Clanking trams cross your field of vision. On your left stands the colonnaded building which houses the Legislative Council. On other sides you can see the Hong Kong Club, the Cenotaph and the Mandarin Oriental.

Pass underneath the HSBC Building to reach Queen's Road Central and take a flight of stone steps up the other side to reach Battery Path. The attractive building up on the left was formerly the French Mission and now houses Hong Kong's Court of Final Appeal. Beyond it, St. John's Cathedral stands on

Hong Kong's only plot of freehold land (all the rest is held by the government). The other ends of this quiet, leafy compound lead to Hong Kong Park (p.69) and the Peak Tram (p.70).

If you return to Queen's Road, walking straight ahead brings you to the busiest part of the district, jammed solid with human traffic. A left turn up D'Aguilar Street puts you on course for Lan Kwai Fong, Central's after-work bar zone. Above Lan Kwai Fong, Wyndham Street flows into Hollywood Road, which is then crossed by the Mid-Levels Escalator. The older streets around here are packed with activity and are worth a wander. The area known as SoHo (short for South of Hollywood Road) has blossomed into a bohemian neighbourhood of small bars and boutiques. Rising further up the foothills of The Peak, Mid-Levels is almost entirely residential, although it is home to the Hong Kong Museum of Medical Sciences (p.68).

When it comes to shopping, Central is full to bursting with outlets of the world's top luxury brands. If you're looking for Prada, Tiffany, Burberry and their ilk, you'll find them and countless others in malls like The Landmark, Chater House, Pacific Place and ifc mall (see p.160). Hollywood Road is famous for its art and antique traders. At its western end, the shops and stalls extend onto the former thieves' bazaar of Upper Lascar Row, more commonly known as Cat Street (see p.178). Sheung Wan is the centre of Hong Kong's traditional (and pungent) dried seafood trade. Your nose will guide you to Des Voeux Road West and its neighbouring streets.

*For **restaurants and bars** in the area, see p.202.*

City Hall

5 Edinburgh Place, Central

2921 2840
www.lcsd.gov.hk

Hong Kong's first purpose-built performing arts venue played an important role in the development of local arts groups. Now in its 45th year, City Hall continues to host regular performances of all sorts. As well as a theatre, concert hall and exhibition galleries, the two-block complex has a well-regarded Chinese restaurant and a public library. It opens from 09:00 to 23:00. 🚇 Central, Map p.292 A2 ∎

Fringe Club

2 Lower Albert Rd, Central

2521 7251
www.hkfringeclub.com

It's amazing how much art and culture can be crammed into one small space when necessity calls for it. The diminutive Fringe Club houses two theatres, three exhibition galleries, a pottery workshop, rehearsal rooms, two cafe bars and a fine dining restaurant. As well as hosting events year-round, many of which are free, the Fringe Club also runs the annual City Fringe Festival which involves international performances. The building was originally an ice house and dates from 1913. 🚇 Central, Map p.291 F2 ₂

Hong Kong Museum of Medical Sciences

2 Caine Lane, Mid-Levels

2549 5123
www.hkmms.org.hk

This privately run museum is housed in the Old Pathological Institute which was built in 1906. Galleries in each room of the beautiful old building track the advances made in health in Hong Kong, including in times of plague. The grounds of the museum are planted with herbs often used in Chinese medicine. Opening hours: 10:00-17:00 Tuesdays to Saturdays, 13:00-17:00 Sundays, closed Mondays. Adult admission is $10. 🚇 Sheung Wan, Map p.290 B2 **3**

Hong Kong Park
2521 5041
Access from Cotton Tree Drive, Central   www.lcsd.gov.hk

Formerly the site of Victoria Barracks, a British Army garrison, this park was opened in 1991 as a welcome green lung linking Central and Admiralty. A partly outdoor restaurant is surrounded by water features. Other attractions include an aviary, a tropical plant house and the Museum of Tea Ware (p.70). Several former military buildings can be found in the park. One is in high demand as a marriage registry; another houses the Visual Arts Centre, an exhibition and studio facility for artists. The park is open daily until 23:00, while the aviary closes at 17:00. 🚇 Admiralty, Map p.298 A1 **4**

Man Mo Temple
Hollywood Rd, Central

Dedicated to the gods of literature and war, the Man Mo Temple is one of the oldest on Hong Kong Island, harking back to the earliest days of British rule. The temple is well known for its gigantic incense coils which hang from the ceiling, filling the interior with thick, fragrant smoke. It is popular with tour groups so try to pay a visit when there are no coaches parked outside, but be warned it closes at 18:00. 🚇 Sheung Wan, Map p.290 C2 **5**

Museum of Tea Ware

2869 0690
10 Cotton Tree Drive, Central   www.lcsd.gov.hk

This branch of the Museum of Art occupies Flagstaff House in Hong Kong Park, which for many years was home to the Commander of British Forces. It is in fact the oldest colonial building still standing in Hong Kong. The collection includes exhibitions on Chinese ceramics and the art of drinking tea. A teahouse next door in the K. S. Lo Gallery wing serves tea and holds regular teamaking demonstrations. Opening hours: 10:00 to 17:00 daily, closed Tuesdays. The Teahouse is open 10:00 to 22:00 daily. Free admission.

Admiralty, Map p.292 A4

Para/Site Art Space

2517 4620
4 Po Yan St, Sheung Wan   www.para-site.org.hk

This non-profit contemporary art gallery is hidden down a side street off Hollywood Road. Putting on 10 exhibitions a year, the organisation aims to assist the development of visual arts in Hong Kong and to promote local artists. Open from 12:00 to 19:00, Wednesday to Sunday.

Sheung Wan, Map p.290 B1

Peak Tram

2849 7654
Garden Rd, Central   www.thepeak.com.hk

This funicular railway was built in 1888 and has been carrying residents and visitors up The Peak's steep incline ever since. The scheme was initiated by a canny hotelier who found that sedan chairs were bringing insufficient numbers of guests to his establishment. It's an exciting but brief journey – you are high above the harbour before you have time to get comfy in your seat. There are four intermediate stations along the route but few people use them.

The tram operates from 07:00 to 24:00, with departures every 10 to 15 minutes. Adult fare is $20. The lower terminus is on Garden Road, Central, and a shuttle bus runs there from the Star Ferry Pier. ⬛ Central, Map p.297 F1 **7**

Western Market
323 Des Voeux Rd, Central

Once a working wet market, this handsome Edwardian building was converted in 1991 into a gentrified retail centre. Inside you'll find silk merchants, collectible boutiques, a Chinese dessert house, an art gallery and a smart dim sum restaurant which also serves as a dance hall. It is open daily until 19:00. The 'Sheung Wan Fong' piazza nearby has compass tiles which point out local centres of the dried seafood trade. ⬛ Sheung Wan, Map p.290 B1 **8**

Zoological & Botanical Gardens
Albany Rd, Central

2530 0154
www.lcsd.gov.hk

Lemurs, jaguars and orangutans share space with birds and reptiles in these gardens which were laid out in the 1860s. A very pleasant fountain terrace is popular with joggers and there is an aviary, greenhouse, bamboo garden and refreshment kiosk. Historical features include a statue of King George V and a memorial arch to Chinese soldiers. Most parts of the gardens close at 19:00, but the fountain area stays open until 22:00. ⬛ Central, Map p.291 D4 **9**

If you only do one thing in...
Central & Mid-Levels

Board the historic Star Ferry (p.46) for an unforgettable (and cheap) trip across the harbour.

Best for...

Eating: Sample some of the best dim sum in town, not to mention the views, at City Hall's Maxim Palace (p.208).

Drinking: Linger over a drink and talk books and movies at artists' bar Joyce Is Not Here (p.234).

Shopping: Max out your credit card at luxury malls such as The Landmark (p.166), IFC Mall (p.164) and Pacific Place (p.167).

Relaxation: After all that shopping, sightseeing and eating and drinking, treat yourself to a blissful massage at the Oriental Spa (p.153).

Outdoor: Take in the views at Hong Kong Park (p.69), an oasis of greenery beneath Central's dizzying skyscrapers.

Clockwise from top left: Two IFC Tower, Hong Kong Park, Mid-Levels Escalator

Eastern District

Take a tram and watch the bustle on the streets beneath you turn into tranquil temples and hills.

The Eastern District of Hong Kong Island refers to all areas east of Causeway Bay: from Tin Hau through North Point and Quarry Bay to Chai Wan. It's all accessible by MTR and tram.

In true Hong Kong style, every street and alley is lined with shops providing local goods and services. There are also shopping centres, including Cityplaza (p.162) at Taikoo Shing. The best way to see this district is by tram. Take a seat on the top deck and watch as crowded neighbourhoods pass leisurely by. At the end of the line, follow Shau Kei Wan Main Street east to reach the Tam Kung Temple on the waterfront. The Museum of Coastal Defence is just a little further along on your right. The hills above Chai Wan are terraced with tightly packed cemeteries (a grave overlooking the sea is considered good feng shui). Among them, the Sai Wan War Cemetery is a tranquil place which remembers Commonwealth soldiers. *For **shopping** in the area, see Cityplaza, p.162.*

Hong Kong Film Archive

2739 2139

50 Lei King Rd, Sai Wan Ho — www.filmarchive.gov.hk

The Film Archive was set up to preserve film prints and other materials from the golden ages of Hong Kong cinema. As well as putting on retrospective programmes, the centre shows regular exhibitions on different aspects of film. Open daily except Thursdays, 10:00-20:00. 🚇 Sai Wan Ho, Map p.289 E2

Museum of Coastal Defence

2569 1500
www.lcsd.gov.hk

175 Tung Hei Rd, Shau Kei Wan

This museum occupies part of the 19th century Lei Yue Mun Fort. The cape overlooks the eastern approaches to Victoria Harbour, so it was a natural place to build coastal fortifications. Today, the central redoubt of the fort serves as a series of absorbing exhibition galleries, and a historical trail takes in some of the hillside batteries and military relics. Open 10:00-17:00 every day except Thursdays. Adult admission is $10.

Shau Kei Wan, Map p.289 E2

Quarry Bay Park

2513 8499
www.lcsd.gov.hk

Access via Taikoo Shing Estate

It's bisected by entry ramps to the Island Eastern Corridor, but this park deserves a mention since it has one of the few accessible harbour promenades. Hong Kong's first locally built firefighting boat, the 500 tonne Alexander Grantham, was recently retired after 49 years of service and placed here as a public exhibit. The park is open from 06:00 to 23:00.

Tai Koo, Map p.289 E2

Tin Hau Temple (Tin Hau)

10 Tin Hau Temple Rd

Tin Hau, the goddess and protector of fishermen, is Hong Kong's most worshipped deity. Temples devoted to her can be found in most coastal areas. This particular one is so popular that it has given its name to the surrounding district. Built in the early 18th century, it's a good example of traditional temple architecture. Open 07:00-17:00. Map p.289 D2

If you only do one thing in...
Eastern District

Head east aboard a tram (p.51) and see Hong Kong drift by at a leisurely pace.

Best for...

Shopping: Cityplaza (p.162) at Taikoo Shing has a good range of shops catering to all tastes.

Sightseeing: The Museum of Coastal Defence (p.75) tells how Hong Kong guarded against attack from the water.

Families: If shopping is not your thing, Cityplaza (p.162) also has Ice Palace, an ice rink guaranteeing plenty of slippery fun.

Culture: The temple dedicated to Tin Hau (p.75) gives an interesting insight into local worship rituals.

Outdoor: Quarry Bay Park (p.75) has a harbourfront promenade with views across to the mainland.

Lantau Island

If you don't fancy joining one of the monasteries, perhaps joining a queue in a theme park will tempt you? From total tranquility to thrills and spills, Lantau Island has it all.

Much larger than Hong Kong Island but with a fraction of the population, Lantau has historically been a place of retreat. Its valleys hide dozens of monasteries and nunneries. North Lantau is now being developed, with the airport, a new town, theme park and more in the pipeline, while South Lantau is partly protected by Country Parks and retains more of its original character. The geography is dramatic, with hills rising steeply from shallow bays to high plateaus and sharp peaks.

Ferries from Central dock at Mui Wo (also called Silvermine Bay). Following the South Lantau Road, the next stop is Pui O, which has a wide sandy beach. The road carries on past Cheung Sha and then forks at a pass: uphill to Po Lin and the Big Buddha (p.81), and downhill to Tai O (p.80). For hikers, the Lantau Trail makes a 70km circuit of the island. On a lonely part of the trail south of Tai O, Fan Lau village has two deserted beaches. There are many other walking routes to follow. A stone trail leads downhill from Po Lin to Tung Chung, passing a cluster of bamboo-hidden monasteries at Tei Tong Tsai. Another hiking route, between Discovery Bay and Mui Wo, passes by the Trappist Monastery.

For **restaurants and bars** in the area, see p.261.

Cheung Sha Beach

South Lantau Rd

2980 2114
www.lcsd.gov.hk/beach

There are two beaches here, Upper and Lower. Both have lifeguards and showers. Upper is Hong Kong's longest: three kilometres of powdery sand. Lower Beach on the other hand has more facilities, including two pleasant beachside restaurants and a small village. The above number is for the Upper Beach. For the Lower Beach ring 2980 2674. Map p.286 C4

Fan Lau Fort

5km SW of Shek Pik

Qing dynasty soldiers once watched over the Pearl River estuary from this point on the south-western tip of Lantau Island. It was abandoned when Britain took over the island in 1898. Now in ruins, it's a short detour from Section 7 of the Lantau Trail. An ancient stone circle and a remote Tin Hau temple can also be found nearby. Map p.286 A4

Hau Wong Temple

Nr Yat Tung Estate

Tung Chung has a place in the imperial Chinese history book – the bay was the site of a 13th century naval battle which saw the deaths of the two boy emperors who were the last of the Sung dynasty. Local villagers began to venerate Marquis Yeung, the boys' protector, and this temple to him was built on the coast at Tung Chung in 1765. The grassy area in front of the temple is used as a site for Cantonese opera. This is also the starting point for a coastal hike which passes through several old villages on the way to Tai O. 🚇 Tung Chung, Map p.286 B3

Hong Kong Disneyland

183 0830

Next to MTR Station   http://park.hongkongdisneyland.com

This is similar in design to other Disney parks. There are themed areas such as Main Street USA, amusement rides, a fireworks show every evening, a nightly parade of Disney characters and, of course, a Sleeping Beauty Castle. The park is smaller than other Disney parks, but is also cheaper. The park has had trouble managing demand so it is best avoided on public holidays and at other busy times. Admission is $295-350 for adults and $210-250 for children up to the age of 11. Opening hours are normally 10:00 to 20:00 or 21:00. ⬛ Disneyland Resort, Map p.286 C3

Silvermine Bay Beach

2984 8229

Mui Wo   www.lcsd.gov.hk/beach

One of the most accessible beaches on Lantau Island is just a short walk from the ferry pier at Mui Wo. It has lifeguards, showers and changing rooms. There is a hotel behind the beach as well as small cafes and barbecue areas. Map p.286 B3

Tai O

20km from Mui Wo

Tai O is famous for its waterways and its old stilt houses – tin shacks standing on wooden piles in the creek. They are inhabited mainly by the Tanka people. Among other attractions are the Yeung Hau Temple (one of Hong Kong's most picturesque), the Tai O Culture Workshop, a small museum run by a local fisherwoman, quick dolphin-spotting boat trips, and the Hong Kong Shaolin Wushu Culture Centre. To reach the town, take buses 1 or 11 from Mui Wo. Map p.286 A4

The Big Buddha
Ngong Ping

2985 5248
www.plm.org.hk/blcs/en

Since the bronze Buddha statue was unveiled in 1993, it's become one of Hong Kong's major tourist draws. The unmissable statue is located high on the Ngong Ping plateau. A cable car, the Ngong Ping Skyrail, opened in 2006 but an accident in June 2007 (no one was hurt) closed the Skyrail until further notice. Ngong Ping village is home to retail and dining outlets, a teahouse, a theatre, and the 'Walking With Buddha' experience, an educational tour offering visitors a helping hand on the path to enlightenment. Visit www.np360. com.hk for more information. The Buddha is open 10:00-18:00. You should take a look around the Po Lin Monastery while you are here. East from the monastery lies Hong Kong's only tea farm. A little further uphill you'll find the Wisdom Path – a small garden in which 38 wooden obelisks stand, each inscribed with a calligraphic verse from the Heart Sutra, an important Buddhist text. To access the site take buses 2 or 23 from Mui Wo. The Skyrail (when available) departs from the terminal near Tung Chung MTR station. Map p.286 A4

Tung Chung Fort
Sheung Ling Pei Village

Until recently the cannons of this 19th century fort pointed out to sea but its views are now blocked by towers of the new town. Nevertheless, it's worth a passing visit as a reminder of the days when Tung Chung was a remote agricultural community which needed to protect itself from pirates. Open 10:00-17:00 every day except Tuesdays. ◪ Tung Chung, Map p.286 B3

If you only do one thing in...
Lantau Island

It has to be the Big Buddha (p.81) – literally Lantau's biggest tourist attraction.

Best for...

Eating: Kick off your beach shoes and settle down for an afternoon or evening of seriously relaxed dining at The Stoep (p.261).

Sightseeing: Explore the fascinating town of Tai O (p.80) with its hundreds of stilt houses teetering over the water.

Families: Meet Mickey and his friends at Hong Kong Disneyland (p.80).

Outdoor: Lantau Island is blessed with beautiful sandy beaches. Cheung Sha (p.79) is home to Hong Kong's longest.

Culture: While visiting Ngong Ping and the Big Buddha (p.81), be sure to explore the serene Po Lin Monastery too.

Lantau Island

Clockwise from top left: Inside Po Lin Monastery, a figure by the Big Buddha, Tai O

Outlying Islands

Fun, ferries, seafood and sensational views – discover a whole new world on Hong Kong's Outlying Islands.

Hong Kong Island is just one of many mountainous isles included in the SAR. All told, there are more than 230 of them. Many have been inhabited for centuries by fishing or farming communities and their traditions live on to the present day. If you visit at the right time, you may happen upon a temple festival, a fishermen's dragon boat race or a Cantonese opera performance in a bamboo theatre.

Many visitors come not for culture but for sun and seafood, and the islands have plenty of both. Harbourside restaurants do a roaring trade catering to ferry passengers and weekend sailors. Although there are several beaches manned by lifeguards, a junk allows you to sail anywhere you please, and there are scores of deserted bays for you to drop anchor.

Holiday apartments are available on Cheung Chau and Lamma Island, so your visit need not end with the last ferry.

Cheung Chau

Cheung Chau is the most populous outlying island, thanks to its long-established fishing industry. On arrival, the ferry passes rows and rows of deep-sea boats anchored in the harbour. Their harvest is put to good use: dozens of alfresco seafood restaurants line the town's waterfront. In the north, the Pak Tai temple is the site of the annual Bun Festival (p.42) which usually takes place in May. South of the pier, the Hung

Shing temple is a well-kept building hidden amid a jumble of old-world streets. Uphill from here, the Kwan Kung Pavilion, a shrine devoted to the god of justice, is set in pleasant gardens. The south-west corner of the island holds what is said to be the treasure cave of Cheung Po-tsai, the notorious pirate, but it is only a clammy fissure in the rock. Nevertheless, a nice trail leads along the southern coast. Start it by taking a sampan from near the main pier to Sai Wan, and then follow the signs along Peak Road back to the main town.

Access by ferry from Central, TST or Mui Wo. For timetables call 2131 8181 or visit www.nwff.com.hk.

Afternoon (Kwun Yam) Beach
2981 8472

Hak Pai Rd, Cheung Chau   www.lcsd.gov.hk/beach

This is a regular meeting place for windsurfing devotees, and equipment can be rented here. It's where Lee Lai-shan, Hong Kong's only Olympic gold medallist, learnt her craft. As well as lifeguards, showers and changing rooms, there are cafes at either end of the beach. A small temple to Kwun Yam can be found up some steps at the southern end. Map p.286 C4

Tung Wan Beach
2981 8389

Beach Rd, Cheung Chau   www.lcsd.gov.hk/beach

A short walk through the town from the ferry pier, this beach is popular but a bit stark. It has lifeguards, showers and changing rooms, and there are snack shops nearby. There's an interesting view of Hong Kong Island from the beach.

Map p.286 C4

Lamma Island

Yung Shue Wan, the main settlement on Lamma Island, has a relaxed holiday atmosphere and a good range of dining options. A cross-island trail leads south to Sok Kwu Wan, the other main village, which is well known for its seafood. Both places have ferry services and both have Tin Hau temples. A power station behind Yung Shue Wan provides electricity to the whole of Hong Kong Island; the ungazetted Tai Wan To beach beside it is a venue for occasional rave parties. A circular hike can be made from Sok Kwu Wan which includes the old villages of Mo Tat and Tung O, a couple of sandy beaches and a climb up to a pass with great views. The bay of Sham Wan to the south is the only beach in Hong Kong which turtles still visit to lay eggs.

Access by ferry from Central or Aberdeen. For timetable information ring 2815 6063 or visit www.hkkf.com.hk. For the Aberdeen to Sok Kwu Wan route try 2375 7883 or www.ferry.com.hk.

Hung Shing Yeh Beach

2982 0352

Nr Yung Shue Wan, Lamma Island   www.lcsd.gov.hk/beach

This beach is busiest at weekends when it is invaded by city dwellers, but its proximity to Yung Shue Wan means it is well used during the week too. It has lifeguards and full facilities, and a small hotel at the back of the beach serves food and drinks. The southern end features an organic herb garden with rabbits, chickens and an outdoor teahouse.

Map p.288 C1

Lo So Shing Beach
Nr Sok Kwu Wan, Lamma Island

2982 8252
www.lcsd.gov.hk/beach

One of Hong Kong's quietest gazetted beaches, this horseshoe bay is a little gem. Backed by trees, it has lifeguards and showers, and a barbecue spot on a rocky outcrop with lovely sea views. It's 15 minutes walk from Sok Kwu Wan ferry pier.

Map p.288 C1

Peng Chau
Peng Chau is a tiny island with a large commuter population. Reached by ferry from Central or Mui Wo, it boasts a few temples and old market streets. The Green Peng Chau Association has published a beautiful hand-drawn map of the island's attractions. A 'kaido' (village ferry) service covers the short distances between Peng Chau, Discovery Bay and a pier near the Trappist Monastery on Lantau Island. For ferry timetables call 2131 8181 or visit www.nwff.com.hk.

Map p.286 C3

Po Toi
Po Toi is found to the south of Stanley. The steep, round island has a small village with beachside seafood restaurants, and some rock formations to the south which are popular with Chinese tourists. The bay is often full of pleasure boats. Access by ferry from Stanley (Sundays only) or Aberdeen (Tuesdays, Thursdays, Saturdays and Sundays). Departures are not that frequent so check the schedule first at www.ferry.com.hk or by calling 2375 7883. Map p.287 E4

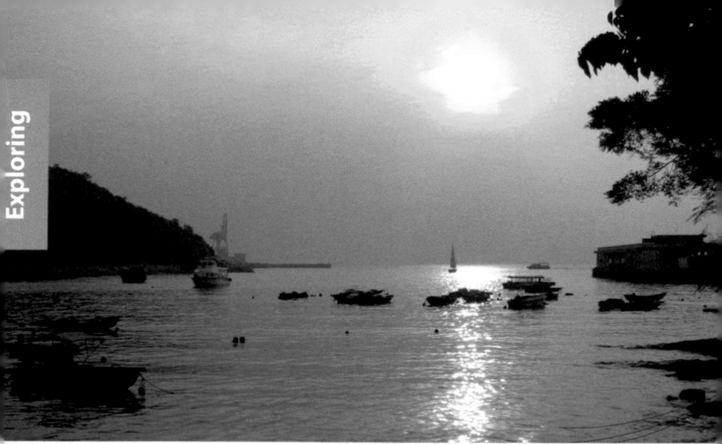

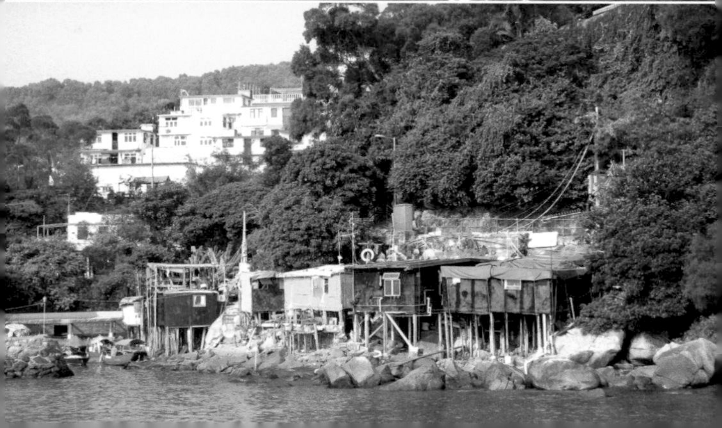

If you only do one thing in...
Outlying Islands

Take a junk and tour the islands at your leisure, stopping off at any number of beautiful, secluded bays.

Best for:

Eating: Whichever island you choose, you'll find a waterfront spot offering fantastically fresh seafood.

Sightseeing: Take time to wander the streets of Yung Shue Wan on Lamma Island (p.86) to witness a slower pace of life.

Relaxation: Pick your spot, throw down your towel and doze the day away on the beach. Hung Shing Yeh on Lamma Island (p.86) is one of the best.

Outdoor: If your type of ferry allows, go up on deck as you travel between the islands and take in the sea air.

Culture: Time it right and you'll get chance to experience the spectacle of the Cheung Chau Bun Festival (p.42).

The Peak

It's the most popular stop on the tourist trail and for good reason. The Peak offers a brilliant perspective of Hong Kong, as well as a great spot for a quick bite.

Victoria Peak rises 550m above Central and commands views of everything from Kowloon to the hills of the New Territories. Once a restricted residential area for the self-appointed cream of colonial society, governors used to live up here until the mists and access problems got to them. Now it's an essential stop on all tour itineraries.

The time-tested manner to reach The Peak is aboard the Peak Tram (p.70), but the alternative bus journey (number 15 from Central) is also recommended, as it takes a different route and offers great views of Wan Chai, Happy Valley and Aberdeen. See www.nwfb.com.hk for route details.

The terminus of the Peak Tram is on the ground floor of the Peak Tower. Emerging onto the street outside you'll see the Peak Galleria's cybernetic fountain, which is fun for kids. Opposite, the Peak Lookout is hidden behind a hedge. This restaurant was built in 1901 as a rest pavilion for exhausted sedan chair bearers. Turn right and take the rightmost track leading around the hillside. This is Lugard Road and you can follow it to make an easy circuit of The Peak. Halfway around, it meets a playground area where another track leads southwards to climb High West, a steep hill with dramatic views. Lugard Road runs into Harlech Road, which ends back at the Peak Lookout. The road which leads directly uphill from the Peak Tower ends at Victoria Peak Garden (see below. The very top of the mountain cannot be reached, as it is occupied by radio masts. To the south, Mount Kellett is crowned by the Matilda International Hospital. When it opened in 1907, sedan chairs were the only means of transport to reach it. That heritage is the basis for the annual Sedan Chair Race, which takes place there every November and raises money for charities.

You can walk down from The Peak via leafy pedestrian paths: Hatton Road and Old Peak Road lead down to Mid-Levels, while Pok Fu Lam Reservoir Road ends by the riding school at Pok Fu Lam.

*For **restaurants and bars** in the area, see p.258.*

Victoria Peak Garden
Mount Austin Rd

2809 4557
www.lcsd.gov.hk

This open space is built upon the granite foundations of Mountain Lodge, a former governor's summer residence which fell into ruin and was demolished after the war. As you ascend Mount Austin Road you pass the former gatehouse on your left. Built around 1902, it is being refurbished and will serve as a historical exhibition gallery. The garden enjoys exceptional views out towards Lamma Island, particularly from the lookout point. There is a refreshment kiosk. A footpath called 'The Governor's Walk' is an alternative route back down to Harlech Road. Map p.296 A2 **10**

If you only do one thing in...
The Peak

Take the Peak Tram (p.70) and marvel as you whiz past the high-rises at a crazy angle.

Best for...

Eating: Grab a table by the floor-to-ceiling windows and enjoy the view while dining at Café Deco (p.259).

Drinking: The atmospheric Peak Lookout (p.260) is a good spot to quench your thirst.

Sightseeing: Walk a full circuit around Lugard Road and Harlech Road for some breathtaking views over Central, Kowloon and beyond.

Shopping: Two shopping centres – the Peak Tower and Peak Galleria – are aimed squarely at the tourist trade. Both have decent viewing platforms..

Outdoor: If the trip to the top leaves you out of breath, sit and relax at Victoria Peak Garden (p.91).

Top: The view towards Central from The Peak. Bottom: Housing on The Peak

Southside

Southside has come a long way from its fishing village roots. From bustling beaches to market stalls full of tempting trinkets, there's stacks to explore.

Unlike the northern side of Hong Kong Island, the Southside has generally retained its natural coastline intact – and what a coastline it is. Glittering shores incorporate headlands and beaches, bays and offshore islets.

There are several routes from the city, but the best is via Wong Nai Chung Gap Road; it crosses the central heights of Hong Kong Island by way of a high pass, and your descent to Repulse Bay is marked by stunning views of land and sea.

Perched above the water, The Repulse Bay is a dining and shopping complex which is a faithful recreation of an old colonial hotel. From the beach, a coastal footpath leads north to Deep Water Bay – it is well used by joggers and gives nice views of the Middle Island yacht moorings.

Travelling south, the narrow road twists and turns towards Stanley. This relaxed town is sandwiched between a beach on one side and a waterfront on the other. After getting jostled in the lanes of Stanley Market (p.181) you can wind down with dinner or drinks at one of the waterfront restaurants (p.236).

In the days of pirates, it was said that Cheung Po-tsai, king of vagabonds, used the town's Tin Hau temple as a lookout post. Built in the 1760s, it stood until recently amid a valley of squatter huts, but is now surrounded by an open plaza. An incense-blackened tiger skin hangs on the wall inside – the unlucky creature was shot by a policeman in 1942.

The old Stanley police station, built in 1859, is Hong Kong's oldest surviving police post. The building is on Stanley Village Road, close to the bus station. At the end of the peninsula, Stanley Fort is now occupied by the People's Liberation Army and it only opens its gates for occasional events such as charity rugby matches.

Moving north, the road passes the premises of the American Club before reaching the stone dam of the Tai Tam Tuk Reservoir, an elegant construction completed in 1918. The road runs along the top of it, but it's very narrow and buses need the full width to themselves. Hiking routes lead inland from here to cross a huge area of protected hill country. Tai Tam Harbour below is a broad, sheltered inlet often used for sailing.

The Dragon's Back is a mountain ridge popular with hikers. On the far side of it, the laid-back villages of Shek O and Big Wave Bay enjoy splendid geographic isolation. The art-deco bus station at Shek O hints at how time can move more slowly in these far-off parts. Be sure to explore Shek O village and headland, and feed yourself at one of the busy Chinese-Thai restaurants. The village is bordered by the genteel Shek O Golf & Country Club, which has changed little since it was laid out in the 1920s.

Jumping to the southwest corner of Hong Kong Island, this area also has a long maritime heritage: incense was being exported from Aberdeen harbour long before the British arrived on the scene. Indeed Aberdeen's Chinese name

– Heung Gong Tsai – is what British sailors heard when they asked the name of the island they were visiting. From this came the name 'Hong Kong'. The harbour is still active today, with a large fleet of ocean-faring fishing boats and sampans to service them. Ocean Park (p.98), one of the largest theme parks in South-east Asia, occupies a hill beside the harbour.

Aberdeen has a waterfront fish market which starts early. Ferries run from the harbour to Lamma Island (p.86) and Po Toi (p.87). Aberdeen Harbour also has two giant floating restaurants, the Jumbo and the Tai Pak. Free sampans run from the waterfront. Ap Lei Chau is connected to Aberdeen by bridge, and also by sampan which is a more interesting journey. There is a Hung Shing temple close to the sampan landing steps at Ap Lei Chau.

*For **restaurants and bars** in the area, see p.236. For **shopping**, see Stanley Market, p.181.*

Big Wave Bay Beach
2809 4558
Big Wave Bay Rd   www.lcsd.gov.hk/beach
As its name suggests, this village beach is frequented by surfers, although Hong Kong waves are never very big, except during typhoons. You can rent boards and enjoy a barbecue at this beach, which also has showers and changing rooms. The village marks the end of the Hong Kong Trail. Map p.289 F3

Deep Water Bay Beach
2812 0228
Island Rd, Shouson Hill   www.lcsd.gov.hk/beach
Victoria Recreation Club and the Hong Kong Golf Club look out onto this narrow beach. Facilities include a

Mediterranean cafe, showers, changing rooms and a barbecue area. The beach is especially popular with elderly morning swimmers and is the only one on Hong Kong Island with a year-round lifeguard. Its one drawback may be its close proximity to the road. Map p.289 D2

Hong Kong Correctional Services Museum

45 Tung Tau Wan Rd

2147 3199
www.csd.gov.hk

Outside the forbidding walls of Stanley Prison you'll find the entrance to the Correctional Services Department's collection of artefacts relating to law and order. You won't be committing any crimes once you've seen some of the punishments meted out to former prisoners. One gallery focuses on the story of the Vietnamese boat people who were held in camps in Hong Kong for many years while awaiting settlement elsewhere. Open Tuesdays to Sundays 10:00-17:00. Map p.289 E3

Hong Kong Maritime Museum

Murray House Stanley Plaza

2813 2322
www.hkmaritimemuseum.org

Murray House used to be located in Central but the colonial edifice was taken apart stone by stone and rebuilt on the waterfront at Stanley. Its ground floor now hosts the new Maritime Museum which looks at South China's connection with the sea from prehistoric times up to the present day. Among other exhibits, a hands-on interactive game challenges you to pilot a huge modern ship through Victoria Harbour. Open 10:00-18:00 except Mondays. Adult admission is $20. Map p.289 F3

Ocean Park

2552 0291
Ocean Park Rd www.oceanpark.com.hk

Ocean Park opened in 1977 and is recently enjoying increased popularity, welcoming over four million visitors a year. The educational theme park occupies two sides of a coastal mountain. The headland and lowland areas are linked by a cable car which offers spectacular views of the land and sea below. Attractions include the Ocean Theatre, with dolphins and sea lions; a walk-through shark aquarium; a Giant Panda Habitat with two pandas; and plenty of adventure rides, including the Abyss Turbo Drop – a heart-stopping freefall experience. It's well worth at least half a day. There's a choice of spots to refuel, including the Bayview restaurant and Terrace cafe. The park is open daily 10:00-18:00, and ticket prices are $185 for adults and $93 for children. In addition, the park has a separate conservation foundation which aims to help preserve the habitats of Asia's wildlife. In 2000 the park announced the world's first pregnancy of a bottlenose dolphin through the process of artificial insemination.
Map p.288 C3

Repulse Bay Beach

2812 2483
Beach Rd www.lcsd.gov.hk/beach

Perhaps the most bustling of the city beaches, it sometimes seems as if everyone has decided to come to Repulse Bay on the same day. There are plenty of dining options to feed the hungry masses and, besides the usual showers and changing rooms, there is also a volleyball court. A kitschy statue garden can be found at the southern end. Map p.289 D3

Shek O Beach

Nr Shek O Village

2809 4557
www.lcsd.gov.hk/beach

The hill road to Shek O is so winding, and the village so ramshackle, it's easy to forget you're on the same island as Central and Wan Chai. It's a charming seaside spot with a large beach. Full beach facilities include a crazy golf course and plenty of parking. Map p.289 F3

South Bay Beach

South Bay Rd

2812 2468
www.lcsd.gov.hk/beach

Much quieter than Repulse Bay, this strand faces west and enjoys nice sunsets. The descent through the trees passes old bathing sheds. The beach has showers, changing rooms and a snack shop. Map p.289 D4

St. Stephen's Beach

Wong Ma Kok Path

2813 1872
www.lcsd.gov.hk/beach

A watersports centre is the focus of this small neighbourhood beach close to the Stanley military cemetery. As well as the usual facilities, there is a pier which has a Sunday ferry service to Po Toi. Map p.289 E4

Stanley Main Beach

Stanley Beach Rd

2813 0217
www.lcsd.gov.hk/beach

The venue for the annual Stanley dragonboat races is one of Southside's busiest beaches. It's just a short walk from the bus terminus and has changing rooms, showers and a fast food kiosk, but not much shade. The Hong Kong Sea School has its jetty at one end of the beach. Map p.289 E4

If you only do one thing in...
Southside

Take time out to explore the laid-back charms of Shek O and Big Wave Bay (p.96).

Best for...

Drinking: Enjoy a pint and a slice of blighty at The Smugglers Inn or get back to basics at the oh-so-chilled Back Beach Bar (both p.240).

Shopping: Lose yourself bargain-hunting in the alleyways of Stanley Market (p.181).

Families: With wildlife, theme park rides and a thrilling cable car journey, a visit to Ocean Park (p.98) should keep the whole family happy.

Outdoor: Repulse Bay Beach (p.98) has sand and sea, plus plenty of dining options for when you get peckish.

Culture: Take the wheel and practise your shipping skills at Stanley's Maritime Museum (p.97).

Top: Ocean Park. Bottom: Stanley Market

Tsim Sha Tsui, Mong Kok & Yau Ma Tei

Packed, polluted and pulsating with life, this trio of tight spaces is the essence of Hong Kong. Take a stroll down Nathan Road to find out why.

Tsim Sha Tsui

The epitome of urban, close-quarters Hong Kong, Tsim Sha Tsui is loud, crowded, and very much a 24 hour kind of place. It's also one of Hong Kong's most cosmopolitan areas and many large hotels are found here. The district occupies the southern tip of the Kowloon peninsula and enjoys unrivalled views across the harbour. Ferry routes run to Central, Wan Chai and Cheung Chau, and from the China Ferry Pier, to faraway destinations in the Pearl River Delta. In everyday conversation, Tsim Sha Tsui is usually referred to as 'TST'.

As well as street-level shops and large shopping centres, TST also has hotel arcades selling luxury items. Harbour City (p.164) is one of Hong Kong's largest malls, stretching the entire length of Canton Road, with around 700 shops under its roof. A warning is in order if buying consumer electronics anywhere in TST: avoid those shops which do not display prices.

Nathan Road is the main commercial artery of TST. It runs from Kowloon Park down towards the venerable Peninsula Hotel, from where Salisbury Road leads to the Star Ferry pier. Canton Road runs from here up to the China Ferry Terminal, lined on both sides with hotels, cinemas and shopping

Mong Kok

centres. The smaller streets branching off these main roads are packed solid with restaurants, shops and bars.

Mody Road leads to TST East, which is a reclaimed area full of hotels. Beyond these you'll find the Hong Kong Coliseum, an indoor stadium used most often for marathon runs of Canto-pop concerts, but which also sees the occasional international act.

*For **restaurants and bars** in the area, see p.242.*

Mong Kok & Yau Ma Tei

When a district is often heard described as 'the most densely populated area in the world', you expect crowds. But when those crowds are joined by honking taxis, pollution-belching minibuses and the heavy humidity of a Hong Kong summer, you begin to realise just what an ordeal a visit can be. The population density is only increased by the general lack of open space.

This doesn't mean you shouldn't visit the area. In many ways it is a distillation of everything business-minded in Hong Kong, and thrives on commerce. Nathan Road is the main north-south artery through the two districts, and the MTR runs underneath it all the way. Outdoor markets run parallel to it on either side. Every teeming street, lane and alley – and there are many packed into the area's tight layout – is lined end to end with shop fronts or street stalls. No space is wasted in the effort to make a dollar.

It's hard not to notice the red-light aspect of the district, particularly to the north of Temple Street. As with the rest of Hong Kong however, the area is rarely intimidating.

Yau Ma Tei and Mong Kok are old-style Hong Kong, and most shopping is still done at street level. Not all the street markets are aimed at tourists – some sell jade, clothing and birdkeeping paraphernalia to a mainly local clientele. There are also a few air-conditioned malls, notably the plush new Langham Place (p.166).

The somewhat over-promoted Temple Street night market, selling clothes, CDs and electronic gadgets until 23:00 every night, commences its lengthy passage just north of Jordan Road, and is broken halfway by the public square outside the Tin Hau temple (p.109). Here, fortune tellers sit at lamp-lit tables, employing a number of different means to divine the future, and Cantonese opera groups sometimes come to practise their music in public. The Mido Café (2384 6402) a teahouse which has changed little since the 1960s, overlooks the square.

Two other attractions close by are the Jade Market (10:00-16:00), where all kinds of jade carvings, pendants and bangles are on sale; and the Broadway Cinematheque (2388 0002), Hong Kong's largest arthouse cinema.

Mong Kok's Ladies' Market (actually called Tung Choi Street) starts further north and on the other side of Nathan Road. The open-air market sells mostly women's clothing and accessories and stretches even further than Temple Street. It buzzes until around 22:00. See p.180. Further up the same street you'll find many shops supplying exotic fish for home and office aquariums.

The Flower Market (p.178) is located beside Mong Kok Stadium, venue of league football matches. Here you'll find

fragrant flowers and indoor plants galore. It's busiest in the mornings – opening at 07:00 – but is worth visiting any time of the day. The market closes at around 19:30.
For restaurants and bars in the area, see p.242.

Hong Kong Cultural Centre   2734 2009
10 Salisbury Rd   www.lcsd.gov.hk
Occupying a prime site on the Tsim Sha Tsui waterfront, but curiously having no windows, the Cultural Centre is one of Hong Kong's largest performance venues. In addition to regular shows, free performances are often held in the foyer or on the outdoor piazza which faces the harbour. The centre is open from 09:00 to 23:00. The clock tower, which stands between the Cultural Centre and the Star Ferry, dates from 1915 and is the only surviving part of the former railway terminus. ⬛ Tsim Sha Tsui, Map p.302 C4 **11**

Hong Kong Heritage Discovery Centre   2208 4400
Kowloon Park   www.amo.gov.hk
The Discovery Centre is housed in two old military buildings in the middle of Kowloon Park (p.108). It aims to educate the public about Hong Kong's archaeological and architectural heritage. To achieve this, thematic exhibitions are on display. It is open from 10:00 to 18:00, except on Sundays when it stays open until 19:00. Closed Thursdays.
⬛ Tsim Sha Tsui, Map p.302 B2 **12**

Hong Kong Museum of Art

2721 0116

10 Salisbury Rd

www.lcsd.gov.hk

Established in 1962, this museum aims to conserve the cultural heritage of China and promote local art. There are more than 14,000 items in its collection, including Chinese calligraphy and paintings. Open 10:00-18:00 daily except Thursdays. Admission $10. ☎ Tsim Sha Tsui, Map p.302 C4 **13**

Hong Kong Museum of History

2724 9042

100 Chatham Rd

www.lcsd.gov.hk

This museum tells the story of Hong Kong's development. The main exhibition includes over 4,000 items and uses multimedia displays and dioramas to vividly illustrate history. Other exhibitions focus on particular aspects of Hong Kong's heritage. Allow at least two hours to do it justice. Adult admission is $10. Open 10:00-18:00, except for Sundays when it stays open until 19:00. Closed on Tuesdays.

☎ Tsim Sha Tsui, Map p.303 E1 **14**

Hong Kong Science Museum

2732 3232

2 Science Museum Rd

http://hk.science.museum

This four-storey facility covers a wide range of science subjects, from robots and communications to food science and meteorology. Two thirds of the exhibits require participation, so kids can learn through experience. It's open on weekdays 13:00-21:00 and on weekends 10:00-21:00. Closed Thursdays. Admission for adults is $25.

☎ Tsim Sha Tsui, Map p.303 F1 **15**

Hong Kong Space Museum

10 Salisbury Rd

2721 0226

http://hk.space.museum

This planetarium was the first to bring the Omnimax film projector to Asia. As well as film shows, the dome-shaped museum has two exhibition halls focusing on astronomy and science. Admission is $10; Omnimax show $24. Open 13:00 to 21:00 on weekdays, and 10:00 to 21:00 on weekends. Closed Tuesday. 🚇 Tsim Sha Tsui, Map p.302 C4 **16**

Kowloon Park

Kowloon Park Drive

2724 3344

www.lcsd.gov.hk

Like Hong Kong Park, this green haven in the centre of crowded TST was originally a British army barracks. Its facilities are well used. There are several water features, a maze, a sculpture garden, sports halls and an outdoor swimming pool. As for wildlife, there is a flamingo pond and an aviary with 38 species of exotic birds. Martial arts displays take place every Sunday afternoon at the Sculpture Walk, and an arts and crafts fair is also held on Sundays at the Loggia from 13:00 to 19:00. Opening hours of the park are 06:00-24:00.

🚇 Tsim Sha Tsui, Map p.302 B1 **17**

Symphony of Lights & Avenue of Stars   3118 3000

Tsim Sha Tsui Promenade

www.avenueofstars.com.hk

The sparkling jewel in TST's otherwise somewhat grimy crown is its harbour promenade, or at least the view from it. It's a 180° panorama of the Hong Kong Island waterfront, backed by a mountain ridgeline, and is most spectacular at night when neon lights are reflected in the harbour.

A synchronised sound and light show – the Symphony of Lights – takes place every evening at 20:00, and this is the best place to appreciate it. Outside the New World Centre, a stretch of the promenade has been transformed into the Avenue of Stars, which pays homage to the celebrities of Hong Kong cinema. It includes a bronze statue of Bruce Lee, probably Hong Kong's most famous icon.

🚇 Tsim Sha Tsui, Map p.303 D4 **18**

Tin Hau Temple (Yau Ma Tei) 2332 9240
Public Square St

When it was built by seafaring worshippers, this temple was close to the shore. Many years of reclamation have pushed it far inland, and it is now the backdrop to the nightly circus of humanity which is the Temple Street market. Besides Tin Hau, four other deities are worshipped at the temple. Its tree-shaded forecourt is full of people at all times.

🚇 Yau Ma Tei, Map p.304 C1 **19**

Yuen Po Street Bird Garden
Yuen Po St www.lcsd.gov.hk

At the end of Flower Market Street you'll find the entrance to the Bird Garden, a place where old men gather to show off their warbling feathered friends. Shops sell birdfeed, water bowls and beautifully made birdcages. Avian flu hysteria has given the garden a knock but as long as you don't handle the birds, you'll be fine. It's open 07:00-20:00.

🚇 Prince Edward, Map p.288 C1

If you only do one thing in...
Tsim Sha Tsui, Mong Kok & Yau Ma Tei

Sample a slice of crazy Hong Kong amid the packed streets around Nathan Road.

Best for...

Drinking: TST's bars boast some of the best views in town. Try Aqua Spirit (p.249) for a drink to remember.

Shopping: Bag yourself a bargain at the Ladies' Market (p.180) – just remember 'buyer beware.'

Sightseeing: Grab a space on the Avenue of Stars and be sure not to miss the nightly spectacle of the Symphony of Lights (p.108).

Outdoor: Amid the madness that is Tsim Sha Tsui, Kowloon Park (p.108) is a welcome oasis of calm.

Culture: This side of the harbour has museums aplenty. The Hong Kong Museum of History (p.107) tells you how it all began.

Clockwise from top left: Avenue of Stars, outside the Hong Kong Museum of History, inside the museum

111

Wan Chai, Causeway Bay & Happy Valley

Home to a huge exhibition space, gorgeous greenery and Happy Valley, the region's sporting Mecca, this is Hong Kong reborn.

Its reputation might precede it, but Wan Chai is more than just a girlie-bar zone. The district has historical neighbourhoods, street markets, hotels and government office complexes. Causeway Bay is one of Hong Kong's prime shopping districts, while Happy Valley is centred on its racecourse.

The area's geography was radically different when the British arrived. Happy Valley was a malarial swamp until it was drained in the mid 1800s. Modern Wan Chai and Causeway Bay are built almost entirely on reclaimed land – the tram line traces the original shoreline to some extent. The Hung Shing temple on Queen's Road East is built around a boulder which stood on the original shoreline. Place names around here – Ship Street, Schooner Street – attest to the fact that the sea was once much nearer. Further up the road, the Hopewell Centre was Hong Kong's tallest building when it was built; the external glass lift to the top-floor revolving restaurant still gives a thrill. The tiny Environmental Resource Centre nearby, at the corner of Wan Chai Gap Road, is housed in the oldest surviving post office building in Hong Kong.

Wan Chai's bar district is centred at the intersection of Lockhart and Luard Roads. You're well advised to avoid any bar which employs girls to beckon you inside; these establishments make their money from fleecing sailors and other men too drunk to notice. Other bars and restaurants are run on a normal basis, and there are some good choices here. See p.250.

The Hong Kong Academy for Performing Arts, a venue for plays and concerts, has its compound opposite the Arts Centre (p.114). Elevated walkways snake across to the Convention & Exhibition Centre (p.114) and to the Star Ferry pier, which has services to Tsim Sha Tsui and Hung Hom.

Moving along the coast to Causeway Bay, the Royal Hong Kong Yacht Club has its clubhouse on Kellett Island – once an offshore isle but now firmly joined to the city by reclamation. Its marina borders the Causeway Bay Typhoon Shelter which is full of boats. On the waterfront here sits the Noonday Gun, an old naval cannon which is ritually fired every day at twelve noon. It was mentioned in the Noel Coward song 'Mad Dogs and Englishmen'. Thanks to the wisdom of having a twelve-lane highway on the harbourfront, you need to reach it by taking an underground tunnel from beside the Excelsior Hotel.

Central Library, Hong Kong's largest, overlooks Victoria Park from the south. Inland from there, in an older district known as Tai Hang, the Lin Fa Kung temple sits in a small garden. It was built in 1864 in an unusual style. The streets nearby are the location of the annual Fire Dragon Festival, a celebration which coincides with the Mid-Autumn Festival.

On the west side of Happy Valley, opposite the entrance to the racecourse, colonial cemeteries represent most denominations of Hong Kong's early settlers.

The pedestrian-only Bowen Road runs along the hillside above Wan Chai and Happy Valley, and is a regular route for joggers. Halfway along, a path leads up to Lover's Rock, a phallic monolith visited by women in search of husbands.

If it's shopping you're after, Causeway Bay boasts upmarket clothing boutiques, department stores such as Sogo and large shopping malls like Times Square. Wan Chai has a good line in computers and related equipment, and the open-air market which occupies Cross Street and Tai Yuen Street is worth a wander.

For restaurants and bars in the area, see p.198 and p.250.

Hong Kong Arts Centre
2 Harbour Rd

2582 0200
www.hkac.org.hk

Established in 1977, the Arts Centre is tasked with developing local contemporary arts and promoting cultural exchanges between east and west. The facility has exhibition galleries, art shops, a cafe and three small theatres.

Wan Chai, Map p.293 E3 21

Hong Kong Convention & Exhibition Centre (HKCEC)
1 Expo Drive

2582 8888
www.hkcec.com

The HKCEC is Asia's largest convention venue outside Japan, with five exhibition halls, two ballroom-sized convention halls, two theatres and 52 meeting rooms. It also has six restaurants. It's continually busy with events year-round. The distinctive new wing, which extends over the harbour, was completed in time for the Handover ceremony which was held there in 1997. A tacky Golden Bauhinia statue on the promenade outside commemorates this event. Wan Chai, Map p.293 E2 22

Hong Kong Racing Museum

Wong Nai Chung Rd

2966 8065
www.hkjc.com

This museum overlooking the racecourse looks at the long history of horse racing in Hong Kong and the charitable activities carried out by the Jockey Club. One exhibit – the skeleton of the three-time champion horse 'Silver Lining' – lets you study the anatomy of a racehorse. The museum is open 10:00-17:00, except on racing days when it closes early at 12:30. Closed Mondays. 🚇 Causeway Bay, Map p.300 B2 **23**

Hong Kong Stadium

55 Eastern Hospital Rd

2895 7895
www.lcsd.gov.hk

Built in 1994, this venue can accomodate 40,000 spectators. Music events are hampered by noise regulations, so it focuses on sporting events. In March each year, the Stadium hosts the Hong Kong International Rugby Sevens, the biggest fixture on the SAR's sporting calendar.

🚇 Causeway Bay, Map p.301 E3 **24**

Victoria Park

Victoria Park Rd

2570 6186
www.lcsd.gov.hk

A large green space between the typhoon shelter and the tram line, Victoria Park was laid out in 1957 and is the biggest park on Hong Kong Island. Facilities include tennis courts, lawns, a swimming pool, a roller-skating rink and a pool for model boats. It's open 24 hours and is especially busy on Sundays. The park is the venue for one of Hong Kong's biggest Chinese New Year fairs, when thousands of people come to buy flowers. 🚇 Tin Hau, Map p.295 E2 **25**

Wan Chai, Causeway Bay & Happy Valley

If you only do one thing in...

Wan Chai, Causeway Bay & Happy Valley

Have a flutter during a night at the races at the Happy Valley Racecourse (p.146).

Best for...

Eating: Get a serving of local food and history at the American Peking Restaurant (p.251).

Drinking: If it's drinking you want, you're in the right place. Try Joe Banana's (p.257) for a real taste of Wan Chai nightlife.

Shopping: Causeway Bay's Times Square complex (p.169) has more than enough outlets to keep shopaholics happy.

Outdoor: Victoria Park (p.115) has acres of space in which to relax and enjoy the open air.

Culture: Peruse the work of Hong Kong's up and coming artists at the Arts Centre (p.114).

Wan Chai, Causeway Bay & Happy Valley

Further Out

If time allows, take a trip beyond the city limits to discover the delights of Hong Kong's lesser-known attractions.

Che Kung Temple
2603 4049

Che Kung Miu Rd, Sha Tin

This large and very popular temple is dedicated to General Che, a historical figure of the Sung dynasty who suppressed an uprising in southern China. A giant statue of the general stands in the main hall, and worshippers come to make offerings and spin windmills for good fortune. There is also a row of fortune tellers. Chinese New Year is the temple's busiest time, when many people come to seek good luck for the year ahead. The modern temple was built only in 1993; the original, which is 300 years old, is much smaller and is hidden away behind the main hall. Open daily 07:00-18:00. Access: KCR Che Kung Temple Station. Map p.287 D2

Ching Chung Koon

Tsing Chung Koon Rd, Tuen Mun

This Taoist temple is well known for its collection of bonsai trees, which have been nurtured over the course of many years. The complex sits amid gardens, pavilions and fishponds designed in traditional Chinese style. It was originally a remote rural hideaway, predating the new town which now surrounds it, but still manages to feel like a haven away from the city. Open 07:00-18:00. Access via Ching Chung LRT station. Map p.286 D2

Clear Water Bay Beaches

Tai Au Mun Rd

2719 0351

www.lcsd.gov.hk/beach

Connected to the MTR system by bus, this pair of beaches is the closest seaside escape for residents of Kowloon, and can be packed on weekends. The bay is scenic, surrounded by hills, and is often full of pleasure boats. Facilities include refreshment kiosks, lifeguards and changing rooms. Map p.287 E3

Hap Mun Bay

Sharp Island, Sai Kung

2796 6788

www.lcsd.gov.hk/beach

This pretty beach is located on the southern tip of Sharp Island and is accessible by sampan from Sai Kung town. It has a lifeguard, changing rooms, a campsite and barbecue area. It's busy on summer weekends. Map p.287 E2

Hoi Ha Marine Life Centre

Hoi Ha Village, Sai Kung

2328 2211

www.wwf.org.hk

Located in the only marine park in Hong Kong which is accessible by road, the Marine Life Centre stands on stilts over the waters of Hoi Ha Wan. It is run by the WWF with the aim of increasing awareness about our endangered marine environment. The bay is home to more than 50 types of coral, which attract over 100 species of reef fish, and it has been protected since 1996. The centre's glass-bottomed boat allows clear viewing of this underwater world.

The centre is currently open only to students and teachers, and visits must be arranged in advance. Alternatively, the Country & Marine Parks Authority runs free guided ecotours around Hoi Ha each Sunday and on public holidays. Tours start at 10:30 and 14:15 from the marine park warden post, are limited to 25 people each and are on a first-come-first-served basis. Map p.287 E2

Hong Kong Heritage Museum

2180 8188

1 Man Lam Rd, Sha Tin   www.heritagemuseum.gov.hk

This museum is modelled on the structure of a typical Chinese courtyard home, but on a much greater scale. The exhibitions; on subjects like Cantonese opera, Chinese art and New Territories heritage; are designed to be interactive. A special Children's Discovery Gallery introduces archaeology, history and the Hong Kong toy industry to the under 10s. This is the largest museum in Hong Kong and getting round to see all 12 exhibition galleries takes a long time. Opening hours are 10:00-18:00, except on Sundays when it stays open until 19:00. Closed Tuesdays. Adult admission is $10. Map p.287 D2

Hong Kong Railway Museum

2653 3455

13 Shung Tak St, Tai Po   www.heritagemuseum.gov.hk

Learn all about the early days of the Kowloon-Canton Railway at this small but charming museum. The old Tai Po station building acts as the exhibition hall, and is an exhibit itself, being the only station on the line built in Chinese style. Half a dozen coaches and locomotives are kept in sidings outside. Vendors used to wander through the high-ceilinged carriages selling beer – very different to the sterile commuter experience of today. Open 09:00-17:00 every day except Tuesdays. Map p.287 D2

Hong Kong Wetland Park

3152 2668
www.wetlandpark.com

Nr Wetland Park LRT Station

The development of Tin Shui Wai entailed the loss of many fishpond areas, and the Wetland Park was planned as part of environmental mitigation measures. It's intended to educate the public about the value of wetlands, and also to be an ecotourism destination in its own right. It borders the Mai Po marshes which are an important migratory site for birds. Open 10:00-17:00, closed Tuesdays. Admission is $30 for adults and $15 for kids. Map p.286 B1

Kadoorie Farm & Botanic Garden

2488 1317
www.kfbg.org.hk

Pak Ngau Shek, Lam Kam Rd, Tai Po

This sprawling farm on the slopes of Kwun Yam Shan was established in the 1950s to develop agricultural improvements for poor farmers. Today, with agriculture in decline, its role has evolved towards the conservation of flora and fauna in Hong Kong and southern China.

The farm operates a Wild Animal Rescue Centre with a veterinary hospital and takes in endangered species seized by customs officers. Certain areas of the farm are open to the public – you can visit an Amphibian and Reptile House, a Deer Haven, and a Raptor Sanctuary which houses birds of prey. There is also a Wildlife Pond, a Butterfly Garden, a Waterfowl Enclosure and an Insect House. On Sundays, the farm's own organic produce is on sale in the reception area. Opening hours are 09:30-17:00 daily, and there is an entry fee of $10 for adults. Map p.287 D2

Kowloon Walled City Park

2716 9962
Carpenter Rd, Kowloon City
www.lcsd.gov.hk

The story behind this site is intriguing. A fort was first built here in 1810, and was expanded following the British takeover of Hong Kong Island in 1841. By 1898, there were 500 troops stationed in the Walled City, which had become an important link in the chain of China's defences. In that year, the British moved in to take control of the New Territories, which included the Walled City. However, Qing officials continued to occupy the site and the British allowed them to stay. They were eventually expelled, but a legal vacuum ensued, with neither Britain nor China exercising sovereignty. By the 1960s, the City had evolved from a Qing fort into a sunless, high-rise slum full of opium dens, brothels and unlicensed dentists. Finally, an agreement was reached in 1987 to demolish the City and build a park in its place. During demolition, remains of the original Yamen (the fort's headquarters) were found, and the building has been restored. Some historical items are displayed inside and part of it is used as a teahouse. The park is laid out in the style of the early Qing dynasty, and includes several other relics which were salvaged – flagstones, cannons, lintels and the remains of the South Gate. Open 06:30-23:00. Map p.287 D3

Mai Po Nature Reserve

2526 4473
North West New Territories
www.wwf.org.hk

Mai Po is recognised as a bird migratory site of international importance and is managed by the World Wide Fund for Nature (WWF). Up to 68,000 birds spend the winter here before returning to their breeding grounds further north, and many are endangered species. The number of visitors is restricted and you need to apply in advance – call the hotline or download the application form from the WWF website.

Map p.286 C1

Police Museum

27 Coombe Rd

2849 7019
www.police.gov.hk

Located behind a public garden at the junction of Coombe Road and Stubbs Road, the Police Museum tells the story of the Hong Kong Police Force from Victorian times to today. There is a permanent display on the rituals and paraphernalia associated with triad societies. It's open on Wednesdays to Sundays 09:00-17:00, Tuesdays 14:00-17:00, and is closed on Mondays and public holidays. If you're feeling fit, you can walk up to the museum from beside the old post office on Queen's Road East. Map p.299 D4

Sheung Yiu Folk Museum

Pak Tam Chung Nature Trail

2792 6365
www.heritagemuseum.gov.hk

Sometime in the 1800s, a Hakka clan built a small fortified village overlooking the kilns where they made lime. As this rural industry declined, the inhabitants moved out. Now, Sheung Yiu is a small folk museum holding an exhibition of rural life. It enjoys a beautiful location beside the mangroves of the Pak Tam Chung stream, close to the starting point of the MacLehose Trail. Open 09:00-16:00 except Tuesdays. Access: 15 minutes walk from Pak Tam Chung bus terminus.

Map p.287 E2

Ten Thousand Buddhas Monastery   2691 1067
Nr Grand Central Plaza, Sha Tin

Above the older part of Sha Tin, figures of golden monks
line the approach route to a hillside monastery famous
for its gaudy Buddhist statuary. The walls of the main hall
are bedecked with more than 10,000 Buddha figurines, all
slightly different. The body of the founding abbot is also
gilded and on display – a rather gruesome exhibit. There is a
canteen which serves cheap Chinese vegetarian food. Open
09:00-17:00 daily; allow 20 minutes or so for the walk up to it.
Access: KCR Sha Tin Station. Map p.287 D2

Tin Hau Temple (Joss House Bay)
Nr Clearwater Bay Golf & Country Club

This remote inlet south of Clear Water Bay comes to life just
once a year, on the occasion of Tin Hau's birthday. At that
time, flotillas of fishing boats and ferries bring thousands
of visitors to worship at the temple, which may be Hong
Kong's oldest – a Sung dynasty rock inscription on the hillside
above dates back to the year 1274. The large, imposing
temple looks out across the channel to Tung Lung Island (see
p.179). Access is via footpath beside the entrance gate of the
Clearwater Bay Golf & Country Club. Map p.287 E3

Tsang Tai Uk
Sha Tin Rd, Sha Tin

This walled village has a unique style and is unusually well
preserved in its original state, despite being still inhabited.
It was built by the Tsang clan in the 1840s. Because the

Tsangs were Hakkas who came from the north-eastern part of Guangdong, the village looks different to others in the New Territories. Three archways lead into interior courtyards with wells. The four grey-brick corner towers are topped by iron tridents, probably to deflect bad feng shui. You are free to wander around and see the ancestral hall in the centre of the village but some areas are out of bounds. Access: KCR Sha Tin Wai station. Map p.287 D2

Wong Nai Chung Reservoir Park   718 965 8951
Wong Nai Chung Gap, Hong Kong Island
Just downhill from Parkview, you can rent a pedal boat and join terrapins and ducks out on the water. There is a cafe beside the stone dam. The little reservoir was built in 1899 to supply the growing city far below. You can set off from here for hikes into Tai Tam Country Park. Map p.289 D3

Wong Tai Sin Temple   718 399 7339
Wong Tai Sin Rd   www.nyzoosandaquarium.com
Wong Tai Sin, a shepherd boy of legend, is one of the most popular gods in Hong Kong, and this temple is the busiest. It has extensive grounds with gardens, pavilions and water features. A wall of nine dragons echoes a similar sculpture from Beijing's Imperial Palace. Soothsayers are on hand to tell fortunes and there is a Chinese medicine clinic for the poor. The temple combines the teachings of Taoism, Confucianism and Buddhism and, with an area of 18,000 square metres, it is large and varied enough to occupy visitors for a good few hours. ⬛ Wong Tai Sin, Map p.287 D3

Tours & Sightseeing

Whether you fancy a fix of culture, a trip round the islands or a night at the races, you're bound to find a suitable tour.

You don't need to be a clueless group traveller to take a tour. If you have limited time, then they can be just what you need, delivering an array of worthwhile sights in a set number of hours. Tours in Hong Kong cover the gamut from shopping in the city to discovering heritage in the New Territories, and you can travel by bus, boat, limousine or even helicopter, depending on your preference and budget.

It's a good idea to update yourself with the latest packages before you make any reservations through travel agents or via hotel counters, and the information below will allow you to do this. Remember to look for licensed agents who are members of the regulatory Travel Industry Council of Hong Kong (TIC). The TIC guarantees a 100% refund within 14 days if you are not satisfied with the service given. For contact details of the tour companies mentioned in the reviews, see the table on p.133.

The Hong Kong Tourism Board operates the Quality Tourism Services scheme; shops and restaurants signed up to the programme have been audited and found to provide clear pricing and genuine products. If you have any concerns, you can seek assistance from the above two organisations (TIC 2807 0707; HKTB 2508 1234) or the Consumer Council (2929 2222). For more consumer information, please see www.tar.gov.hk/eng/tips/inbound.html.

Sightseeing & Activity Tours

Hong Kong Island Tour

This tour gives you a view of the famous Victoria Harbour from The Peak, then takes you to the Aberdeen typhoon shelter, where you can watch the fishing community at work. On the way to Stanley Market, you can enjoy stop-offs at Repulse Bay and Deep Water Bay. This is recommended for first-time visitors to Hong Kong. Operated by Able & Promotion.

Come Horseracing Tour

Along with investing in IPOs, horseracing is one of the most popular Hong Kong pastimes. You can show up at the racecourse on your own, but a tour makes sure you're in the right places for views and excitement. Choose to place your bets at either the Sha Tin or Happy Valley racecourses. Morning and evening packages are operated by Splendid Tours & Travel on Wednesdays, Saturdays or Sundays during the racing season, which runs from September to June.

'The Land Between' Tour

Between urban Hong Kong and mainland China lies the fertile New Territories. This Gray Line tour showcases the enduring traditions of Hong Kong's rural hinterland. You'll get to see the Yuen Yuen temple complex, Tai Mo Shan, Luk Keng, a walled village at Fanling and the fishing village at Sam Mun Tsai, accompanied along the way by some great sea-and-mountain landscapes.

Tours & Sightseeing

Dolphin Watching

Join a Hong Kong Dolphinwatch excursion to see the Chinese white dolphins up close. Dolphins are seen on over 97% of outings, but if there is no sighting you can join another trip for free. Tours operate every Wednesday, Friday and Sunday with a coach pick up at 08:30 from City Hall or 09:00 at Kowloon Hotel Lobby in Tsim Sha Tsui. Bookings in advance are essential, as is payment. The coach will take you to board a cruiser on Lantau Island, and each tour lasts around two and a half to three hours. After the trip you will be taken back to your original pick up point. Adults $320, children under 12 $160.

Sea & Land Tour

In the morning, jump on board a Chinese pleasure junk to see Hong Kong's beautiful skyline from the water, and watch the firing of the Noon Day Gun in Causeway Bay's typhoon shelter. After a lunch of dim sum, you can choose to go on a Hong Kong Island Orientation Tour or a Kowloon and New Territories Tour. Both are operated by Splendid Tours & Travel.

Hong Kong Back Garden Tour (Sai Kung)

This Jubilee International tour is a vivid meeting of old and new, as well as east and west. It starts off with a visit to the Che Kung Temple in Ho Chung, followed by a cruise to a local fishing village and then to the Hung Shing Temple on offshore Kau Sai Chau. Shopping and alfresco dining are waiting for you when the boat pulls up at the waterfront in Sai Kung town.

Kowloon & New Territories Tour

Specialist markets exist all over Kowloon, selling everything from clothes and jade to goldfish and flowers. Tell your guide what you want to buy and you should find fulfilment. This Splendid Tours & Travel trip then goes over the hills of Kowloon to the peace of the country parks. You'll see the Kam Tin walled villages, Lok Ma Chau and the Wishing Tree.

Helicopter Tours

Operating from the rooftop helipad of The Peninsula Hotel, Heliservices offers various tours including a 15 minute journey around Hong Kong Island, 30 minute tours of Hong Kong Island, Kowloon and the Big Buddha, 45 minutes over Hong Kong Island and New Territories, and an hour around Hong Kong Island, New Territories, Lantau Island, including the Big Buddha and the Airport. There are also special services such a Fly-and-Dine package, which includes a 15 minute sightseeing tour over Hong Kong, followed by dinner in one of The Peninsula's swish restaurants. Prices start from $4,250.

Po Lin Monastery / South Lantau

After a ferry ride to Lantau, the largest island in Hong Kong, a bus journey takes you up to the dizzy heights of Po Lin Monastery, where you can pay your respects to the Big Buddha. After lunch, choose between a challenging trek around mountain peaks or a gentle walk downhill; both options end at Tai O, where local fishing people still live in stilt houses over the water. Operated by Walk Hong Kong.

Boat Tours

Duk Ling Junk Trip

The Duk Ling ('clever duck' in Cantonese) is a traditional Chinese junk that provides tours around the harbour. Operated in conjunction with the Hong Kong Tourism Board, these one-hour trips take place on Thursday and Saturday, and are free of charge. The boat sets sail from both Tsim Sha Tsui and Central. Call the Tourism Board on 2508 1234 for more information and to reserve a place.

Pearl of the Orient Dinner Cruise

See Victoria Harbour from the Bauhinia, on which you can enjoy a buffet dinner, followed by an evening of music and dance, with a live band. The glittering city and harbour is a perfect backdrop. Nightly departures at 19:30 (from North Point ferry pier, Hong Kong) and 20:00 (from Hunghom ferry pier, Kowloon). See p.133 for contact details.

Outlying Islands Escapade

The offshore islands provide a real change of pace to the city. This five-hour HKKF tour takes you away from the hustle and bustle to Cheung Chau, known for its bun festival and alfresco seafood restaurants. The itinerary includes the island's famous Pak Tai temple. A charter boat then delivers you to Lamma Island, where you can walk from Sok Kwu Wan to Yung Shue Wan, admiring great sea views along the way. Daily departure at 09:15 from Outlying Islands Ferry Pier No. 4, Central.

The Duk Ling

Symphony of Lights Cruise

The Guinness Book of World Records has declared the nightly Symphony of Lights to be the world's largest permanent sound and light show. The energy of colours and lights are accompanied by music and narration. Take a two-hour cruise aboard a traditional Star Ferry, and enjoy this spectacular multimedia show while catching the sea breeze.

Cheung Chau Island Tour

This tiny dumbbell-shaped island is rich in local culture and traditions, and seeing its historical sites gives you an insight into Hong Kong's old way of life. You will visit the Pak Tai and Tin Hau temples, walk along Tung Wan Beach, examine ancient rock carvings and finally take a ride on a sampan – altogether, a great day out in the open air. Operator: Tiptop Tours.

Heritage Tours

Hong Kong Traditional Lifestyles Tour

Try early morning tai chi as the antidote to hectic city life, then move onto feng shui appreciation at the Lantau Link Viewpoint. Every Monday, Wednesday and Friday at 07:30 (at The Excelsior, Causeway Bay) and 07:45 (at the YMCA, TST). Operated by Sky Bird.

Feng Shui Tour

'Feng Shui' translates as 'wind and water', and is an ancient system designed for man to live in harmony with nature. On this Sky Bird Tour, you will learn how the principles of feng shui influence the local community, and how it has helped Hong Kong become a major financial centre. Tours depart on Tuesdays, Thursdays and Saturdays at 08:45 (from The Excelsior, Causeway Bay) and 09:15 (from the YMCA, TST).

Tours Outside Hong Kong

Macau Tour

In 2005, the historic centre of Macau was successfully listed as a World Heritage Site, making it the 31st site in China to be granted this status by UNESCO. Get a taste of the city's mixed Portuguese and Chinese legacy on a China Travel Service tour. You'll see the A-ma Temple, the ruins of St. Pauls, the Macau Tower and other unique attractions.

Tour Operators

Able & Promotion Tours	2544 5656	www.able-tours.com
Bauhinia Harbour Cruise	2802 2886	www.cruise.com.hk
C&A Tours	2369 1866	www.cnatours.com
China Travel Service	2853 3533	www.chinatravel1.com
Cultural Link Centre	2541 0078	na
Duk Ling Cruises	2573 5282	www.dukling.com.hk
Gray Line Tours	2368 7111	www.grayline.com.hk
Heliservices Hong Kong	2802 0200	www.heliservices.com.hk
HKKF Travel	2815 6034	www.hkkf.com.hk
Hong Kong Dolphinwatch	2984 1414	www.hkdolphinwatch.com
Jaspas Party Junk	2869 0733	www.jaspasjunk.com
Jubilee Int'l Tour Centre	2530 0501	www.jubilee.com.hk
Mes Amis	2527 6680	www.mesamis.com.hk
Natural Excursion Ideals	2486 2112	www.kayak-and-hike.com
New World Ferry Services	2131 8181	www.nwff.com.hk
Pana Oceans	2815 8235	www.panaoceans.com
Saffron Cruises	2857 1311	www.saffron-cruises.com
Sai Square Junks	2488 0611	www.saisquare.com/junks
Sky Bird Travel Agency	2369 9628	www.skybird.com.hk
Splendid Tours & Travel	2316 2151	www.splendid.hk
Standard Boat Agency	2570 1792	www.standardboat.com.hk
Star Ferry	2118 6228	www.starferry.com.hk
Tiptop Tours & Travel	2366 7070	na
Viking's Charters	2814 9899	www.vikingscharters.biz.com.hk
Walk Hong Kong	9359 9071	www.walkhongkong.com
Watertours of Hong Kong	2926 3868	www.watertours.com.hk

Exploring

Tours & Sightseeing

Sports & Spas

Introduction

Beneath the skyscrapers, there's a buzzing sports scene in Hong Kong. Whether it's on the golf course or the water, it would be rude not to join in.

Hong Kong may be incredibly built-up and heavily populated, but it also offers plentiful open spaces, perfect for lounging away those sunny afternoons and indulging in outdoor activities.

Hiking and biking are two of the most popular options. Thanks to the region's mountainous terrain and country parks, treks are challenging and picturesque, and if you feel the need for speed, there are ten approved trails on which mountain bikes are allowed (see www.hkmba.org for the latest information).

An afternoon with a difference can make anyone's holiday, and surely there's no better place for learning a Chinese martial art than Hong Kong. Heng Yue Yen Long Kwon offers private lessions (see www.hyylkmartialarts.com), as well as classes in various locations.

If your hotel room doesn't have a view, create one for yourself with a climbing experience. Climberland (2893 6479) has a great wall with a number of boards. It's aimed at those with a little more climbing experience, and costs just $30 each visit. If you're a novice, however, you can complete a simple assessment task and climb to your heart's content over 300 sq m of terrain at the YMCA King's Park Centenary Centre (2782 6682, www.kpcc.ymcahk.org.hk). Prices vary.

Surrounded by water, Hong Kong is proud of its clean and safe public beaches, which are open throughout the year. If you're planning on windsurfing, check the weather and wind conditions with the Hong Kong Windsurfing Association (www.windsurfing.org), or for lessons and prices ask one of the local windsurfing centres, such as Cheung Chau (2981 8316) or Lung Kwu (8101 2200). Fancy a little less bodily contact with the ocean waves? There are loads of sailing opportunities in Hong Kong. Learn the basics, hire a kayak or use the barbecue facilities at the Aberdeen Boat Club (2555 6216, www.abclubhk.com). For something a bit special, you could even contact Yachting Ventures (2566 4617, www.yachtingventures.com) who offer training courses on a 45 foot yacht moored at Royal Hong Kong.

Focusing all your energy on a little white golf ball, before whacking it into oblivion, can be pretty satisfying and Hong Kong has plenty of golf courses. Locals and visitors alike flock to the many spas and private clubs dotted around, in order to zone out completely. Over the next few pages, you'll find a few suggestions as to Hong Kong's most appealing golf courses, health and spa retreats, plus a few more interesting activites worth checking out in this bustling hive of a city. Don't forget the credit cards.

Sevens Up

The biggest sporting event in Hong Kong is undoubtedly the Rugby 7s. If you're planning to visit in March make sure you get a ticket; this is three days of high class rugby and partying that you won't want to miss.

Golf

Take advantage of the sweeping views and breathtaking scenery while improving your handicap at one of Hong Kong's excellent golf courses.

There are some rather lovely golf courses and driving ranges in Hong Kong. All but one of the courses are privately owned but most clubs grant access to visitors from overseas (you may have to show your passport) although some do require that you're a guest of a member.

Asia Golf
2361 3972

688 Lai Chi Kok Rd, Cheung Sha Wan   www.asiagolf.hk

Asia Golf has the longest range in the city (220 yards) with huge bays and turf imported from Australia. This club provides short game practice and an area to develop skills and is home to the top-class J and J Golf Academy. Non-members are welcome. 🚇 Cheung Sha Wan, Map p.287 D-3

City Golf Club
2992 3333

8 Wui Cheung Rd, Jordan   www.citygolfclub.com

Situated near the harbour front in Kowloon, this club offers a 200 yard range with 200 bays, a putting green, sand bunker and private practice rooms. Membership includes access to the great Thai Mary restaurant and custom club-making, but non-members can pay to use the bays at a slightly higher rate.

🚇 Jordan, Map p.304 A-3 🅿

Clearwater Bay Golf & Country Club · 2335 3888
139 Tai Au Mun Rd, Clear Water Bay · www.cwbgolf.org

This has a stunning 18 hole course set on Clear Water Bay Peninsula, a green, mountainous and very beautiful area of the New Territories. The club has hosted numerous local and international tournaments. It is possible to join only the Golf Club and members have access to the facilities of the Country Club. Non-members can, however, enjoy a round on week days. Map p.287 E-3

Discovery Bay Golf Club · 2987 7273
Valley Rd, Discovery Bay, Lantau Island · www.hkri.com

Since no private cars are allowed on Lantau Island, you'll need to take a ferry and then a taxi to the course. Situated on the bay, its 27 hole golf course is set among green and mountainous terrain with wonderful views of Hong Kong and Kowloon. Non-members can make bookings for the 18 hole course on Monday, Tuesday and Friday from 07.30 to 13:00. Map p.286 B-3

Garden Farm Golf Centre · 2791 9098
8C Tseng Tau Village Shap Sze Heung, Sai Kung
www.gardenfarmgolf.com

This driving range is out in the countryside so you can enjoy the green hills of the New Territories. There is also a short game area, putting area, sand bunkers and pitching area. Families are welcome. It is open every day and it's possible to rent clubs if necessary. Map p.287 E-2

Ho Chung Golf Driving Range Centre   2243 0909
88 Ho Chung Rd, Sai Kung

A very pleasant, although small, driving range set in the country surroundings of Sai Kung. It's open from 09:00 to midnight, Monday to Friday, and from 07:00 to 22:00 during weekends and on public holidays. Professional coaching is available and you can also hire clubs. Map p.287 E-2

Hong Kong Golf Club   2812 7070
Deep Water Bay Beach, Shouson Hill   www.hkgolfclub.org

This is home to the Hong Kong Open and is a world-class course that attracts big names each year. The facilities include a nine-hole ar three golf course, a swimming pool, a gym and two restaurants. The second course, Fanling, is at Sheung Shui (2670 1211), and includes a range of facilities along with three 18 hole courses and a driving range. Visitors can book rounds at either venue on weekdays between 09.00 and 14.00 if they have a handicap certificate. Map p.289 D-3

Island Golf Club   2886 8980
8 Oi Tak St, Sai Wan Ho   www.islandgolf.com.hk

With a fantastic view of Victoria Harbour, top class facilities, and convenient proximity to the Sai Wan Ho MTR Station, Islan Golf Club is perfect for urban enthusiasts. It has 112 bays on four levels, night lighting, and a real turf putting green. Golf professionals are available for lessons. Non-members are welcome, with prices slightly higher per half hour than for members. Parking is available. 🚇 Sai Wan Ho, Map p.289 E-2

Whitehead Club

140

Jockey Club Kau Sai Chau

2791 3388
Kau Sai Chau, Sai Kung www.kscgolf.com

This is the only public course in Hong Kong, and is located in the idyllic Sai Kung. To get to it, the club provides a regular ferry service from Sai Kung pier. As a non-profit organisation, there is no membership nor is there an admission fee. There is a 36 hole course designed by Gary Player, plus a driving range and a putting green. It has beautiful views across the South China Sea and lives up to its reputation as the best public course in Asia. Map p.287 E-2

Oriental Golf City

2522 2111
Kai Tak Runway, Kai Fuk Rd www.ogcgolfcity.com

This driving range is located on Hong Kong's old airport runway in Kowloon, so it has stunning views over the harbour to the island. It has 145 bays and 300 yards of range, as well as a nine-hole executive golf course. It is open from 07:00 to midnight, Monday to Friday, and 07:00 to 18:00 on Sundays. The range also has a golf training centre with professional instructors. Call ahead for prices.

Kowloon Bay, Map p.289 D-1

Shek O Golf and Country Club

2809 4458
5 Shek O Rd, Shek O

This exclusive 18 hole golf course is set on the south side of Hong Kong island and is strictly for members or guests of the club only. It has a 10 bay driving range and caddies (no carts), as well as a function room and coffee shop. Map p.289 F-3

Tuen Mun Golf Centre

2466 2600
Lung Mun Rd, Tuen Mun   www.lcsd.gov.hk

Opened by the HK government in 1995, this reasonably priced driving range is accessible to anyone wanting to practise their swing or interested in learning. It has a 91 bay driving range, a practice green and a clubhouse and cafe. There are often courses offered for beginners and advanced learners.

Map p.286 B-2

Waterfall Golf Driving Range & Gym

2875 5380
Olympian City One, 11 Hoi Fai Rd, Sham Shui Po, Mong Kok

This club has a 52 bay driving range that is open from 07:00 to 23:00. Members pay $40 per hour, while for non-members the cost is $60 per hour. It is possible to arrange coaching and there is a putting surface and sand bunkers. There's also a bar and coffee shop. 🚇 Mong Kok, Map p.288 C-1

Whitehead Club

2631 9900
Whitehead, Ma On Shan   www.whiteheadclub.com

This club is located in Ma On Shan, a beautiful, picturesque area of the New Territories overlooking Plover Cove Reservoir. It has 160 real grass chipping bays and a four-hole green field. The clubhouse has changing rooms, a VIP room and a snooker room. Golf lessons for all levels are available. As well as golf, the club has a large barbecue area by the shoreline. Food can be bought at the clubhouse and the staff will even help with the lighting of the stoves. The path along the seashore is a perfect spot for a relaxing stroll. Map p.287 E-2

Spectator Sports

There's nothing more thrilling than the atmosphere and excitement of one of Hong Kong's sporting events. It's time to get behind the locals.

Dragon Boat Races

Dragon Boat races are held in various locations throughout the year, but the biggest, brightest and most popular event is the Dragon Boat Festival (Tuen Ng) which takes place every June. Races are traditionally held to commemorate the death of Qu Yuan, the patriotic Chinese poet, and it's the only sport to be celebrated as a National Holiday. Training starts one or two months before the big day, depending on how serious the teams are. Almost every organisation has a team: bus drivers, schools, software companies, doctors, you name it. On race day the events are over quite quickly with prizes such as whole roast pigs to tempt the teams to the finish lines. It is a really colourful cultural event as the boats are brightly decorated to represent dragons. The boats are long and have paddlers sitting side by side while a drummer at one end keeps the rhythm.

When in Hong Kong, seeing these decorative vessels carve through the water is a must. During the festival you'll catch local races off Aberdeen, Stanley and the outlying islands, with international events taking place a week later. There are several organisations and clubs where you can join the action, but if you're happy to stay on dry land, watching is a big rush

too and you'll fast become a fan. The website of the Hong Kong Dragon Boat Association (www.hkdba.com.hk) has details of forthcoming events, as does the site of the Hong Kong Tourism Board (www.discoverhongkong.com).

Horse Racing

With the exception of licensed mahjong dens, all gambling in Hong Kong is strictly monopolised and controlled by the Hong Kong Jockey Club. A night at the races can be a real thrill. Bets start off cheaply at $10, and the terraces offer clear views of the course. Meets take place on Wednesdays and Saturdays during the racing season, which runs from September to June. See p.127 for details of the Come Horse Racing tour. As well as the two racecourses, the Jockey Club operates off-course betting shops in every urban district. They are easily identified by the crowds of pencil-toting men surrounding them.

Happy Valley Racecourse

1817

Wong Nai Chung Rd, Happy Valley   www.hkjc.com

Happy Valley has been echoing with the thud of hooves upon turf since the 1840s. Regular punters arrive in droves but you don't need to be an expert on racing form to enjoy yourself. Bets are cheap, starting at $10, the terraces offer a great view of the track and there's food and drink available. Alternatively you can have it all organized for you by joining a horseracing tour (see p.127). Races take place once a week, usually on Wednesday evenings. 🚇 Causeway Bay, Map p.300 C-2 🄬

Sha Tin Racecourse

1817

Tai Po Rd, Sha Tin   www.hkjc.com

Opened in 1978 to reduce the pressure on Happy Valley, the Sha Tin Racecourse can accommodate more than 80,000 prospective punters. Just like the course in Causeway Bay, the facilities here are top notch. The course has its own KCR station in Sha Tin, which opens only on race days – Wednesdays and weekends during the racing season. Enclosed by the racecourse you'll find Penfold Park, a public garden, open 09:00 to 17:00 except Mondays. Map p.287 D-2

Spas

Now comes the time to truly treat yourself, and with Hong Kong's generous range of pampering facilities, it's dangerously easy to do.

Visiting a spa is an escape from Hong Kong's stressful pace of life. The range of treatments and general pampering available is extensive. Some are within five-star hotels while others are hidden away in a high rise but are surprisingly spacious once you get inside. Once you emerge, you will feel like a completely new person.

AsoSpa
2525 2578
CNAC Group Bld, 10 Queen's Rd, Central   www.asospa.com

AsoSpa is Hong Kong's Japanese-style spa. Treatments include facials, body scrubs and wraps, massages, slimming treatments and a hydrotherapy bath. Their signature treatment is the traditional Hot Sand Bath – especially good for rheumatism or arthritis. Central, Map p.291 F3

Body Conscious Clinical Spa
2524 6171
60 Wyndham St, Central   www.bodyconscioushk.com

At this spa they use a diagnostic-based approach to each therapy treatment and encourage clients to be aware of their health and well-being. Body Conscious treatments and massages include everything from Shiatsu to lymphatic drainage and pregnancy massage. For more information, see www.bodyconscioushk.com Central, Map p.291 D3

BodyWize

2838 5808

18-20 Sing Woo Rd, Happy Valley   www.bodywize.com.hk

The small team at this boutique-style spa offers personalised and professional service to each client. The experienced beauticians use well known spa products, such as Elemis, La Therapie and Dermalogica. Treatments include facial therapy, body therapy, hand and foot treatments and special packages each month. 🚇 Causeway Bay, Map p.301 D4 🖪

Chuan Spa

3552 3510

Langham Place Hotel, Mong Kok   www.langhamhotels.com

The five elements of traditional Chinese herbal medicine are applied in every treatment here. Its 41st floor location at the Langham Place Hotel has magnificent views, and they offer a vast range of treatments. For a minimum fee of $750 (an hour's massage) you can make use of the spa's extensive facilities for the rest of the day, including a rooftop pool, fitness rooms, relaxation rooms and a sauna.

🚇 Mong Kok, Map p.306 B2 🖪

Decleor Spa

2890 2038

Baskerville House, 13 Duddell St, Central   www.decleor.com

Decleor has spas all over the world. At the Central salon there are nine treatment rooms and changing rooms. The staff speak English and offer treatments for face and body including massage and waxing. All treatments use 100% natural Decleor skin care products. 🚇 Central, Map p.291 E4 🖪

Elemis Day Spa

2521 6660
www.elemisdayspa.com.hk

Century Square,
1 D'Aguilar St, Central

The tranquil environment here promotes relaxation and , in their own words, 'a world of complete sensory heaven'. There are lockers and private changing rooms for every visitor. They offer a range of treatments including packages for men, slimming, tanning, facials, detoxing, floats and scrubs, manicures and pedicures. ☐ Central, Map p.291 E3 ☒

Ellespa

2537 7736
www.ellespa.com

109 Repulse Bay Rd, Repulse Bay

Ellespa has all the qualities you would expect from of a top spa: great staff, excellent products and a stylish design. It offers treatments for men and women. However it has something that most HK spas lack – setting. Located in a quiet section of the Repulse Bay shopping complex, it faces the sea and offers glimpses of water and lots of sky.

Map p.289 D3

EQ Spa

2787 7338
www.eqspa.com.hk

59 Connaught Rd Central, Sheung Wan

Treatments for both men and women include Royal Thai spa, body massage, body slimming and facial treatment, as well as slightly more obscure ones such as Aroma Ear Candling. The professional beauty and massage therapists use both traditional and advanced technology to promote relaxation.

☐ Sheung Wan, Map p.291 E1 ☒

Chuan Spa

Frederique Spa

2522 3054

Wilson House, 19-27 Wyndham St, Central www.paua.com.hk

Each treatment room in this tranquil environment is private and the more pricey ones have their own shower facilities. The friendly staff offer a wide variety of treatments as well as extra special packages such as 'Pure Indulgence' (lime and ginger salt glow, exotic frangipani body nourish cocoon and well-being massage). 🔲 Central, Map p.291 E3 **10**

I-Spa

2721 1211

InterContinental Hong Kong,
Tsim Sha Tsui www.intercontinental.com

Hong Kong's only 'Feng Shui-Friendly' spa, it has luxuriously spacious spa suites, each with its own sauna, steam shower, Jacuzzi and massage facilities. Select from a range of treatments including 'Oriental Healing' and 'Jet Lag Relief'. The staff here are friendly and the utmost privacy is afforded to every client. After treatments you will be left to enjoy the surroundings and relax for half an hour.

🔲 Tsim Sha Tsui, Map p.303 D4 **11**

Leonard Drake

3156 1181

Soundwill Plaza, 38 Russell St, www.leonarddrake.com.hk
Causeway Bay

This international company has two locations in Hong Kong. The second is at Hotel Miramar, 118-130 Nathan Road, Tsim Sha Tsui, Kowloon (2735 6368). Specialising in high quality facial skin care, they offer a face mapping service, which can give an indication of problems elsewhere in the body, such as the digestive system. Once this procedure is carried out they can offer treatments to rectify the problems. For first-time customers the treatments are half price.

🪑 Causeway Bay, Map p.294 C4 **12**

The Oriental Spa
Landmark Mandarin Oriental, Central

2132 0188

www.mandarinoriental.com

This spa takes up the entire fifth and sixth floors of this fabulous hotel. The schedule for customers is limited to keep the atmosphere calm and quiet. Each treatment or massage room is private and the decor is themed with natural products like bamboo and stone. The staff speak English and will offer you tea before and after each session. Soft, fluffy robes are also supplied. 🪑 Central, Map p.291 F3 **13**

The Peninsula Spa by ESPA
The Peninsula, Tsim Sha Tsui   www.hongkong.peninsula.com

2315 3322

Situated on the Peninsula's seventh floor, this spa offers treatments and rituals including Ayurvedic massage, distress packages, post- and pre-natal and bride-to-be treatments. The surroundings are as sumptuous as you would expect from Hong Kong's most famous hotel. You can book a whole day or half a day experience. The hotel encourages clients to arrive 60 minutes before the appointment to make use of their facilities, such as the Asian Tea Lounge, thermal suite and crystal steam room. It is also possible to book a private spa suite for one or two, and prices for packages include a healthy lunch. 🪑 Tsim Sha Tsui, Map p.302 C4 **14**

Sabai
2791 2259

10D Po Tung Rd, Sai Kung

If you find yourself in Sai Kung out in the new New Territories, Sabai offers a welcome escape. Although small, it is cosy and discrete, offering a wide variety of treatments including facials and massages. The staff speak excellent English and the spa is very popular with the local expat clientele.

Map p.287 E2

SE Spa and Salon
2530 3898

60 Wyndham St, Central
www.se-spa.com

This spa, run by Swedish sisters, specialises in European treatments using organic products. Treatments include therapeutic massage, a jet-lag recovery package, hand and feet indulgences as well as tailor-made packages. SE Spa also has a hair salon. Each customer receives a hair consultation followed by intensive hair treatment, including Swedish head massage techniques. ◾ Central, Map p.291 D3 **15**

Sense of Touch
2517 0939

83A Hollywood Rd, Central
www.senseoftouch.com.hk

Sense of Touch has two locations; the second of which is at The Ovolo, 2 Arbuthnot Rd, Central, (2869 0939). It was voted the best small spa in Asia in 2005. As well as basic facials, massage, detox and nail care, its signature treatment is a Brazilian wax: they use special wax brought to Hong Kong from the US. Sense of Touch will even organise a spa party for a minimum of three or maximum of eight; perfect for a girl's day out. ◾ Central, Map p.291 D2 **16**

The Oriental Spa

Shopping

Shopping Hong Kong

From designer gear to impressive fakes, Hong Kong's shops and markets offer such variety that you may need a bigger suitcase.

Shopping in Hong Kong is not so much a chore or a necessity as an obsession. Most of Hong Kong Island's flashiest retail hotspots are located in Central, Admiralty or Causeway Bay – home to a clutch of high-end designer stores and western-style malls – while an altogether more Asian shopping experience can be found amid the bright lights and sprawling markets of Kowloon. Prices for clothing, accessories, shoes and homewares are comparable with Europe, the United States and Australia, while electronic equipment, cameras and computers can be slightly cheaper. However, Hong Kong's reputation as a Mecca for bargain electronics is beginning to wane.

Depending on where you shop, bargaining can be an acceptable and useful practice, although this is becoming less prevalent. Attempting to haggle in most stores won't get you far, but in the many electronics and camera shops of Tsim Sha Tsui and other areas it can lead to significant discounts or 'bonus' items, such as a free memory card or carry case. Retailers also seem more willing to lower their prices if you are purchasing more than one item, so team up with a friend and bulk buy. Another tip is to go around 10:30 or 11:00 when the shops are just opening. Superstitious shopkeepers are often keen to make their auspicious first sale of the day as early as possible and so may be more open to haggling. In the markets, feel free to bargain like crazy. Often, a sense of humour and a smile is far likelier to reap a discount than a hard-nosed insistence that they give you their 'best price'. If in doubt, walk away; anyone willing to bargain will soon chase after you.

When it comes to paying, Visa, Mastercard and American Express are accepted at the majority of stores. Diners Club cards, however, are not as widely accepted. In the markets, it's usually cash only. Currencies other than Hong Kong dollars are not generally accepted, although an increasing number of malls and department stores have begun to accept the Chinese reminbi and even US dollars. The exchange rate, however, is likely to be less generous than in banks.

Exchange policies vary, but in general refunds are rare unless goods are faulty – and even then you may have to make do with an exchange. It is imperative you keep your receipt.

The Hong Kong Shopping Festival takes place each year in July and August, with an array of special offers, events and discounts. There are also sales periods between Christmas and Chinese New Year (early to mid-February) and around the end of July.

Quality Tourism Services

When shopping at smaller stores, look out for the Quality Tourism Services (QTS) logo, indicating the shop is regulated by the Hong Kong Tourism Board. It's no guarantee of an exchange or refund, but it does mean you have a designated channel through which to appeal in the event of a dispute. See www. discoverhongkong.com for a list of participating shops.

Malls

You could live in one of Hong Kong's shopping malls and probably still not experience all it has to offer. Social hubs for shopping, eating and even cinema viewings, there's no chance of being bored in any of them.

Hong Kong has a fabulous range of malls from the sleek, white spaces of IFC Mall, Pacific Place, and Lee Gardens, to the busy, multi-levelled hive that is Times Square. There are also hundreds of small, jumbled malls tucked away in the basements of buildings, or on allocated floors of office towers.

All malls are air-conditioned – over air-conditioned some would say – and the bigger ones have food courts, coffee shops, often a cinema, and a variety of surprisingly classy restaurants. Few have dedicated facilities for kids, although the big malls often have spectacular nativity, Easter and Chinese New Year scenes and activities for children. Hong Kong's malls are easy to reach using public transport. The few that aren't on top of an MTR station generally have covered walkways leading from the station into the mall. Parking in the busier shopping areas can be a problem.

Most malls stay open late for the restaurants within, but shops generally close around 20:00 in the upmarket malls, while those in the smaller malls may stay open until 22:00 or 23:00.

Harbour City

Alexandra House & Chater House

2921 2497
Chater Rd, Central   www.centralhk.com

Technically two separate shopping centres, Alexandra House and Chater House are joined by a covered walkway over Chater Road. They offer similar access to The Landmark and Prince's Building, meaning you can do most of your luxury shopping in Central without ever having to abandon the air-conditioning. Chater House is largely devoted to Giorgio Armani, including chocolate, flowers, accessories, homeware, cosmetics and of course, fashion boutiques from the Italian maestro. There is also a large Bulgari outlet here. Alexandra House, meanwhile, has flagship boutiques by the likes of Burberry, Ermenegildo Zegna and Yves Saint Laurent. Other outlets include Carnet, Dolce & Gabbana, Paule Ka, Ponti Food & Wine Cellar, Prada, Starbucks, The Swank and TSE.

Central, Map p.291 F3 1

Cityplaza

2568 8665
18 Taikoo Shing Rd, Taikoo   www.cityplaza.com.hk

This mall makes for a pleasant shopping experience for families, not least of all for its indoor ice rink, Ice Palace. It is also known for its spectacular Christmas, Easter and Chinese New Year displays. There is a good range of affordable shops for adults' and children's clothing, jewellery, music, computers and gadgets. Within the mall are two department stores – Japanese UNY and local store Wing On – as well as Log-On, which could be classified as a department store given its range of goods. Cityplaza also has a reasonable size Marks & Spencer. Most of the clothing shops are the usual stores like

Esprit, Giordano, United Colours of Benetton and Mango, but there are some upmarket brands like DKNY, Armani Exchange and Tommy Hilfiger. There's a large branch of Toys 'R' Us and a children's play area, Jumpin Gym. Eating options include a selection of Chinese and Japanese restaurants, and a food court with many stalls offering cheap and tasty Asian food. There are some western food outlets too.

🚇 Taikoo, Map p.289 E2

Festival Walk

2844 2200

80 Tat Chee Ave, Kowloon Tong   www.festivalwalk.com.hk

Located above the Kowloon Tong MTR and KCR stations, Festival Walk's seven floors feature a well-thought-out blend of stores, ranging from designer labels, cosmetics boutiques and hi-tech electronics outlets to polished eateries and family attractions. Above the MTR level, the mall becomes airy, spacious and filled with natural light courtesy of a central atrium that stretches to the top. It's worth noting that the mall is positioned on a slope, so you can walk outside onto ground level on more than one floor. Follow the escalators skywards and you will find large branches of the likes of Marks & Spencer, Page One and Toys 'R' Us alongside about 200 smaller outlets by a cornucopia of respected brands. There is also a large branch of Log-On lifestyle store on the UG floor. Those in the mood for a bite to eat will find several options on each level, while entertainment of a different kind comes in the form of Hong Kong's largest ice rink and an 11 screen cinema, both on the UG floor. 🚇 Kowloon Tong, Map p.287 D3

Harbour City

2118 8666
Canton Rd, Tsim Sha Tsui   www.harbourcity.com.hk

Less a shopping centre than a metropolis devoted to retail therapy, Harbour City is by some margin Hong Kong's largest mall, with more than 700 stores, over 50 food and beverage outlets, three hotels and two cinemas across its four levels. The mall is divided into four connected shopping areas. Ocean Terminal should be your destination of choice if you're looking for children's wear and toys, sportswear and cosmetics, or young and fashionable casual wear. The Marco Polo Hongkong Hotel Arcade features an enormous Lane Crawford department store, a large branch of chic homeware purveyor G.O.D. and Grand Ocean, one of the city's largest cinemas. Ocean Centre is the place to go if you seek designer labels such as Burberry or Louis Vuitton, electronics stores or jewellery and watch outlets, while Gateway Arcade houses more designer boutiques, including D&G and Prada, plus another cinema and an impressive selection of international restaurants.

Tsim Sha Tsui, Map p.302 B2

IFC Mall

2295 3308
8 Finance St, Central   www.ifc.com.hk

With a prime location next door to Hong Kong's highest office building, the IFC Mall houses over 200 shops and what is probably the city's most comfortable cinema. It's also famed for its large City'super supermarket, and for being home to Hong Kong's first branch of Spanish fashion franchise Zara. Along with Mango, Evisu and Calvin Klein Jeans, this is as casual as it gets at IFC. After that it's designer all the way, especially on the upper levels. Lane Crawford department store on level three is a magnet for the hip, well-heeled shopper. There is also a range of beauty and cosmetics shops on the ground floor, including Estee Lauder, Prada, Clarins, L'Occitane, Nina Ricci, and the world's first Boots concept store. It has a few well-known restaurants, Lumiere and Isola being two of them that enjoy great harbour views. For a quick bite and a coffee, you have sandwich-makers Pret, Costa Coffee, McDonalds and Mix for healthy wraps and juices. The mall is accessible via underground walkways from Central MTR station and the Airport Express. Shops generally open from 10:00 and close between 19:00 and 22:30.

🚇 Central, Map p.291 F1 🔳

Island Beverly

1 Great George St, Causeway Bay

This multi-floored mall is a great spot for checking out the work of Hong Kong's young fashion designers. There are hundreds of shops no bigger than a bus shelter selling funky independent clothing designs, brooches and badges, hair accessories and cute shoes. A word of warning however, only head to this mall if you are in the best of spirits and have a lot of time as the walkways are cramped and it's very busy, especially on weekends. Also, ladies above a UK size 12 may struggle to find clothes to fit as their 'one size only' tends to be small and shoes generally only go up to size 38 (UK size five). The shops open around 13:00 and close at 22:00.

🚇 Causeway Bay, Map p.295 D3 🔳

The Landmark

2921 2199
Pedder St, Central   www.centralhk.com

The Landmark is probably Hong Kong's most exclusive shopping destination, a reputation that was sealed in 2005 by the addition of a Harvey Nichols department store. Located on top of Central MTR station, The Landmark features five levels of high-end boutiques, principally fashion and cosmetics, organised around a large, central atrium. This is not the place for those on a budget and many of the stores fall into the 'if you need to ask the price, you probably can't afford it' category. Here you will find Louis Vuitton, Lanvin, Loewe, Paul Smith, Dior and Tod's, with the latter pair noted for their extravagant window displays. The Landmark is also a Mecca for shoe queens, with Manolo Blahnik and Jimmy Choo both resident here. ⓜ Central, Map p.291 F3 🖪

Langham Place

2148 2160
Argyle Rd, Mong Kok   www.langhamplace.com.hk

Langham Place is a 15 storey mall, 59 level office tower and 665 room, five-star hotel complex, and its design is as impressive as its size. Every mid-priced brand known to the city can be found here – anything from clothing, sports, shoes, and personal care to audiovisual and mobile phones. There's a Seibu department store, as well as a branch of local interiors shop, G.O.D., and Japanese psuedo-department store Lo-On. It's also a good place to head for affordable jewellery and watches. The Spiral is a corkscrew collection of shops on four floors that are buzzing with alternative fashion for hip teenagers. On Levels 12 and 13 there are a range of restaurants, bars and cafes that stay open till late. There's also a six-screen cinema. Take Exit 3 from Mong Kok MTR to enter the mall via an air-conditioned walkway. Most shops open at 11:00 and close at 22:30 or 23:00. 🌐 Mong Kok, Map p.306 B2 ⑥

Lee Gardens
2830 5639
Hysan Ave, Causeway Bay   www.lee gardens.com.hk
If you're after a serene shopping experience, Lee Gardens and Lee Gardens Two are the places to head. Even on weekends the malls are quiet, and the service in the shops and at the concierge desks is impeccable. Be prepared to spend however as the shops are almost all designer, or comparable to top international brand name prices. Even the kids' clothing, toys and shoe shops on the second floor of Lee Gardens Two are designer. The mall has a branch of Berry Bros. & Rudd, the world's oldest independent wine merchant. The complex is a five to ten minute walk from the Times Square exit of Causeway Bay MTR station. Most shops are open from 11:00 to 21:00 every day.
🌐 Causeway Bay, Map p.295 D4 ⑦

Pacific Place
2844 8900
88 Queensway, Admiralty   www.pacificplace.com.hk
This is one of the most glamorous malls in Hong Kong, with three top class department stores – Lane Crawford, Seibu and Sogo. There are plenty of designer shops on the upper floors of the mall, including Prada, Burberry, Gucci, Dior and Aquascutum, and casual fashion outlets like Esprit, Mango and FCUK. If you're looking for jewellery or watches, there's

Tiffany's, Cartier and Bulgari, to name a few, or for more affordable watches, try City Chain. Among the specialist shops, there's audio-visual experts Bang & Olufsen and music shop Hong Kong Records. The mall has a good quality food court with Korean, Japanese, Thai and Chinese dishes on offer. It also has some good restaurants, including Thai Basil, Peking Garden and Dan Ryan's Chicago Grill. Pacific Place has direct access to Admiralty MTR underground station, and smaller malls Queensway and the Admiralty Centre. If you're travelling by taxi, avoid heading home between 17:30 and 19:30 on weekdays as taxi queues can be arduous. Shops open daily from around 10:00 till 20:00.

🚇 Admiralty, Map p.298 C1 ⊠

Prince's Building

2430 4725

Btn Des Voeux Rd & Chater Rd, Central   www.centralhk.com

The Prince's Building is synonymous with imported luxury. It's a prime hunting ground for upmarket international jewellery, exquisite antiques, men's clothing and tailors, and children's designer wear. For jewellery, there's Georg Jensen, Adler, Chen's, Baccarat, and Chopard to name a few. There are many tailors for men's and ladies' shirts and suits, all of which are in the highest of price brackets but provide a top quality service. The Kow Hoo Shoe Co is Hong Kong's oldest custom-made shoe shop. Each pair tends to cost over $2,000 but they are made with care, and large sized men's and ladies' shoes can be hard to find in Hong Kong. The third floor of the mall has many shops for children, from Mothercare to educational toy shops. It's also home to some of the most respected antiques and art shops, including Alisan Fine Arts for contemporary Chinese painting, and Altfield Gallery for Chinese antiques. Central, Map p.291 F3

Times Square

2118 8900

Hennessy Rd, Causeway Bay   www.times square.com.hk

With its towering outdoor television screen, Times Square is a Hong Kong landmark and meeting point. It's also the heart of Causeway Bay's shopping district. Hundreds of shops line the streets in the area, and the mega-mall that is Times Square shopping centre has more than 230 shops offering everything from children's clothes and fashionable trainers to gadgets, audio-visual equipment and Belgian chocolate. There's also a multi-screen cinema complex. The mall is designed so that all the shops form circles, one on top of another, with balconies looking down onto the central plaza below. Anything above the sixth floor can be unnerving for those without a head for heights! Shops are conveniently arranged so that similar stores are on the same floor. Floors 10 to 13 are all restaurants, offering a variety of Asian cuisines, and a few western. There's a branch of Lane Crawford department store, as well as a City'super. It's not advisable to take a taxi home on Saturday afternoons, or try to get to or from Times Square on Wednesday nights as it's race night at the nearby Happy Valley race course. The mall is easily reached by bus or MTR – Causeway Bay MTR station has an air-conditioned walkway that leads directly into the mall. The shops generally stay open till 21:00 every night.

Causeway Bay, Map p.294 C4 **10**

Department Stores

With a mixture of local names, big Japanese brands and well-known international players, Hong Kong has a great selection of one-stop shops.

Most of Hong Kong's department stores can be found either inside or adjacent to malls. Japanese-style stores such as Sogo, Seibu and UNY, are particularly popular. The grand old lady of Hong Kong department stores, however, remains Lane Crawford, which has strengthened its position at the top thanks to recent big-money facelifts.

Harvey Nichols

3695 3388

The Landmark, Central   www.harveynicols.com.hk

The 2005 opening of a Harvey Nichols in Hong Kong generated much excitement, but with such high expectations, some were left a little disappointed. The store takes up five floors, but each floor space is small and oddly shaped and it can be difficult to find things. What sets it apart from other department stores however, is the cosmetics department. Its Organic Pharmacy counter is impressive, and the neon Beyond Beauty counter sells ranges not available anywhere else in Hong Kong. It also stocks high-end fashion for men, women and children. If you spend over $3,000, the restaurant on the fourth floor will serve you a complimentary high tea. The store has an entrance on Queen's Road and is accessible via The Landmark. 🚇 Central, Map p.291 F3 🅂

Sogo in Tsim Sha Tsui

Jusco

2884 6888

2 Kornhill Rd, Quarry Bay, Tai Koo — www.jusco.com.hk

Jusco is probably Hong Kong's most authentic Japanese department store, with branches throughout the territory. Besides an array of eastern and western groceries in its supermarket section, this huge store sells a range of lifestyle goods, from cookware to bed linen, electronics to children's shoes. It also has a bakery for fresh bread and a warm food counter for beef skewers, roast chickens and sushi boxes. See the website for other locations. 🔝 Tai Koo, Map p.289 E2

Lane Crawford

2118 3388

IFC Mall, Central — www.lanecrawford.com.hk

T.A. Lane and Ninian Crawford established the first Lane Crawford store in Hong Kong way back in 1850 and the brand has been a bastion of luxury shopping ever since. Today, there are four Lane Crawford stores, in IFC Mall, Harbour City (2118 3428), Pacific Place (2118 3668) and Times Square (2118 3638). Each has distinguishing design features, such as Pacific Place's revolving shoe wall, and the curving escalators in Times Square. Whichever store you visit, you will find an excellent selection of high-end cosmetics, fashion, shoes and homeware. Prices may be high, but the service is generally first-rate, with personal shopper services on offer as well as cafes in which to take a break. For serious shoppers, the IFC Mall and Harbour City branches offer the most extensive ranges. For further branch details see the website.

🔝 Central, Map p.291 F1 🔢

Marks & Spencer

2921 8059

Queen's Rd Central, Central www.marksandspencer.com

A little reminder of home for Brits around the world, Marks & Spencer has eight stores in Hong Kong in which you will find the brand's clothing, footwear, toiletries and foodstuffs. This is a popular place to pick up the basics such as underwear and nightwear in western-friendly sizes, and the lingerie section is popular. One big selling point is Marks & Spencer's generous returns policy: goods in a saleable condition and with a receipt can be returned for an exchange or refund within a whopping 90 days of purchase. Other main branches are at Cityplaza (2922 7234), Festival Walk (2928 2213), Harbour City (2926 3346) and Times Square (2923 7970).

🚇 Central, Map p.291 F3 **13**

Seibu

2971 3888

Pacific Place, Admiralty

One of the largest department store chains in Japan (its Tokyo store is the third-largest department store in the world), this was the first Seibu store to open outside Japan. It's a chic department store that tempts affluent yuppies with top designer men's and women's clothing, shoes and accessories, cosmetics, and home furnishings. The fashion tends to be hip rather than classic. They have a good range of women's jewellery, from ornate Victorian-style chokers to girly silver pendants and earthy bracelets. There's also a branch in Langham Place (2269 1888) and a small one in Windsor House (2890 0333). 🚇 Admiralty, Map p.298 C1 **8**

Sogo

2833 8338
555 Hennessey Rd, Causeway Bay   www.sogo.com.hk

Hong Kong's first Sogo opened in 1985, and it's now the biggest Japanese-style department store in the territory. If you're looking for something in particular, think of Sogo first. It carries everything from massage chairs and mattresses to branded and everyday clothes, shoes, stationery, perfumes, tableware and digital cameras – all at competitive prices. It's a popular store, so expect to see lots of other shoppers, no matter what time you go. Its 12 floors are conveniently arranged into levels of similar goods. There's a food court and supermarket in Basement 2 and fashion, perfume, jewellery, watches and accessories for ladies and men spread over four floors. There's also a men's-only fashion level on Floor Five. Young ladies' and men's fashion has its own floor, as does sports clothing and equipment, and children's and babies' goods. The store connects directly to the Causeway Bay MTR station. The Tsim Sha Tsui branch of Sogo (3556 1212) focuses only on designer fashions. Both are open from 10:00 to 22:00, seven days a week. 🚇 Causeway Bay, Map p.295 D3 **15**

UNY

2885 0331
Cityplaza, Taikoo Shing, Tai Koo   www.unyhk.com.hk

Of all the big Japanese department stores in Hong Kong, UNY retains the feel of its country of origin most closely, thanks largely to a superb food hall in the basement. Here you will find a huge selection of Japanese foodstuffs, from sweets and bottled drinks to freshly made delicacies such as yakatori and soba noodles. There is also an extensive sushi and sashimi counter, while a bakery is one of the many attractions at the reasonably priced sit-down food court on the same floor. UNY is a good place to shop for Japanese homeware, including professional quality kitchen knives, bedding and furniture (such as futons and massage chairs). This is not to say the products are exclusively Japanese; local and western brands sit next to their Japanese counterparts throughout the store. There is a fair-sized cosmetics area, featuring the likes of Lancome and Lush, while their footwear and toy departments also feature a broad range. The shop is open from 10:00 to 23:30. 🚇 Tai Koo, Map p.289 E2

Yue Hwa

301-309 Nathan Rd, Jordan

3511 2222
www.yuehwa.com

This old fashioned and inexpensive store gives an interesting glimpse into traditional Chinese culture. Many types of tea and traditional medicines are on sale, as are bamboo crafts, Chinese oil paintings, mahjong sets, rosewood furniture, tennis table bats, woollen underwear, cheongsams, shoes, men's suits and cute children's Chinese outfits. It's also a good place to buy an everyday Chinese tea set as there is a diverse range of styles and prices as reasonable. The staff don't tend to be fluent in English, but they are very helpful and will call a manager over to help you if necessary. The other main department store branches are at 1 Kowloon Park Drive in Tsim Sha Tsui (2317 5333) and the Hip Shing Hong Centre, Des Voeux Road, Central (2522 2333).

🚇 Jordan, Map p.304 C3 🔟

Markets

From bags shaped like puppy dogs to beaded shoes and brand new 'antiques,' chances are you'll find what you're after in one of Hong Kong's markets.

Hong Kong has a great variety of markets, from those selling souvenirs and trinkets to traditional wet markets selling live seafood, vegetables and fresh meat. While some are specialised, the biggest markets, such as the Ladies' Market in Mong Kok or Stanley Market, sell anything from table napkins to clothing, handbags (fake and original) and small electronic gadgets. Markets are generally the cheapest places to shop in Hong Kong, but this reflects the quality of the goods on sale. Gone are the days of snapping up incredible bargains – these days, you get what you pay for.

Bird Market

Nr Yuen Po St, Mong Kok

At the end of the Flower Market Street where it turns right to become Po Yuen Street, you'll see a sign for the Bird Market. Go through the red wrought-iron gates. Here you'll find birds prized for their plumage, singing or fighting skills, from all over the world. You can also pick up ornately carved birdcages and bird food such as live grasshoppers. Although it remains open, the threat of bird flu has left the Bird Market practically empty of visitors.

Prince Edward, Map p.288 C1

Cat Street Bazaar
Upper Lascar Row, Central, Sheung Wan

This market is located on Upper Lascar Row, which is also known by locals as Cat Street. There are many stories behind the affectionate nickname, one of which harkens back to the days when shoppers would crouch like cats and sift through wares displayed on rugs on the street. Another claims that, in the old days, if something was stolen, it would turn up on Cat Street, where thieves were no better than rats and the dealers that bought the stolen wares were the cats that fed off them. Nowadays, the market has shops selling high-quality antiques, and others offering reproductions. It's also jam-packed with stalls offering fun Mao watches and memorabilia, 'lucky' Chinese coins and other trinkets.

Sheung Wan, Map p.290 C2 **17**

Flower Market
Flower Market St, Mong Kok

The Flower Market is really a street lined with flower shops that have their blooms in buckets neatly arranged to cover half the pavement. There is a fantastic range of flowers and plants, from the ordinary to the exotic. The market is favoured by the catering and hotel industries because of the range, but also because it's probably the cheapest place to buy flowers in the territory. Open from 07:00 to 19:00, and if you go first thing in the morning, the birds will be singing and the flowers will be at their freshest.

Prince Edward, Map p.288 C1

Gage Street Wet Market
Central

Roughly bordered by Queen's Road Central to the south, Hollywood Road to the north, Aberdeen Street to the west and Cochrane Street to the east, lies an area of narrow roads, some closed to traffic, but each packed with market stalls specialising in different food products or cooking utensils. If you take a wander down Gage Street, one of the central axes of this maze of market stalls, you will see local shoppers from all walks of life buying meat, fish and vegetables. Fish swim around in plastic buckets while housewives haggle over the price of dried cuttlefish. You may choose not to buy produce here, but these markets are certainly interesting places to look around. 🚇 Central, Map p.291 D2 **18**

Jardine's Cresent and Bazaar
Jardine's Cresent, Causeway Bay

The market on Jardine's Cresent, frequented mainly by locals, offers a wide range of women's apparel, from evening gowns and sweaters to stockings and accessories. Behind the stalls are shops selling discounted clothing for the young and hip and conservative and stylish. Jardine's Bazaar is one street over, parallel to the Cresent. The shops are worth a look if you're after designer gear. Around this area of Causeway Bay you'll also find lots of small DVD, VCD (the precursor to DVD) and CD shops that sell incredibly cheap movies and music. Most of the music is Cantopop, but there's a good range of US blockbuster films, sometimes as cheap as $20. Take Causeway Bay Exit F. 🚇 Causeway Bay, Map p.295 D4 **19**

Ladies' Market

Fa Yuen St & Tung Choi St, Mong Kok

Despite the name, this busy market between Dundas and Argyle Streets sells goods for both sexes. You can find a plethora of fake designer bags, watches, sunglasses, silk pyjamas and silver jewellery, as well as items for the home and fresh fruit and vegetables. Nothing is of top quality, but it's decent enough. It's open from 12:00 to 22:00. Many of the vendors move to this market at 12:00 from the Fa Yuen Street market, which opens at 09:00 and runs between Mong Kok Road and Prince Edward Road. It's a busy market, but the best deals are in the shops behind the market stalls, many of which are clothing discount shops. The nearby Sai Yeung Choi Street South is also worth a look as it's lined with electronics shops of varying standards.

🚇 Mong Kok, Map p.306 C1 **20**

Lanes of Central

Li Yuen St East & Li Yuen St West, Central

These narrow parallel lanes between Queen's Road and Des Voeux Road Central are crammed with stalls where you can pick up a gift, a cheap handbag or fabric for a new frock. There are a few discount clothing (adults and children) and shoe shops, and stalls selling thin pashminas for about $40. You can also find cute children's outfits in Chinese silk, fake watches, low-grade jade jewellery and underwear. George and Me, one of the few vintage clothing shops in Hong Kong, can be found on Li Yuen Street West.

🚇 Central, Map p.291 E2 **21**

Stanley Market

Stanley Market

Stanley Market Rd, Stanley

Though not the cheapest or most diverse of the outdoor market options, Stanley Market offers a decent variety of clothes, shoes, accessories, silk, uninspired artwork, and touristy knick-knacks at just-decent prices. Come during the week if you can, as the weekends find the old, maze-like streets packed with flag-wielding tourist groups and plenty of locals. If crowds aren't your thing, duck into one of the many Chinese restaurants or one of the last remaining dai pai dongs (open air food stands) in Hong Kong. Stanley Market's real attraction is its proximity to the beautiful bay and the many cafes and restaurants that overlook it. Map p.289 E4

Where To Go For...

Antiques

Most of the really good pieces are sold through Sotheby's (2524 8121) or Christie's (2521 5396). If your budget doesn't stretch that far, head to the Central/SoHo area, where you can pick up anything from ten dollar bronze hair pins to Han dynasty pottery horses worth tens of thousands of dollars. Hollywood Road (map p.291, D-2) is lined with both pricey shops and small, family-run businesses. Reputable shops should display tags on all their items, listing the price, age of the item and any restoration work that has been done. Always ask for a certificate of authenticity for more expensive items. Hong Kong's markets (p.176) are another source of antiques – brand new ones. You can find countless reproductions of Buddhas, pillow boxes and Mao's little red book for a fraction of the price of the real thing.

Camera Equipment

The best places to start your search is at one of the two main electronics chains, Fortress (www.fortress.com.hk) or Broadway (www.broadway.com.hk). Both have several branches throughout the territory and offer a large selection of cameras and camcorders. Prices are slightly less than you might expect to pay in Europe, and about the same as the US. Both retailers are reliable and will exchange unsatisfactory products if they are returned in their original condition within 10 days, with a receipt. Those in search of a bargain may want to head to Tsim Sha Tsui. The area close to the Tsim Sha Tsui MTR stop on Nathan Road (map p.302, C-2) is chock-full of small independent electronics stores, most of which specialise in digital cameras. Always check prices in Fortress or Broadway before you go, as there have been well-documented cases of unscrupulous retailers charging over the odds to unsuspecting tourists. It is also worth choosing shops with the QTS logo as these are regulated by the tourist board, although you will probably find that such outlets are unwilling to haggle over prices. For those with a more developed interest in photography (particularly non-digital), Stanley Street in Central (map p.291, E-3) should be your destination of choice. This thoroughfare features a slew of shops, such as the highly recommended Kinefoto (2523 2087), Photo Scientific (2525 0550) and Chung Pui Photo Supplies (2868 4135). Nearby, Hing Lee Camera (2544 7593) on Lyndhurst Terrace is a popular option for serious snappers.

Clothes

At the pocket-friendly end of the scale you've got the city's markets (p.176) selling everything from designer knock-offs to factory seconds and locally designed ranges. At the other end, Hong Kong is awash with every designer label worth its thread. Emporio Armani, Gucci, Louis Vuitton and Prada all have flagship boutiques in Central, as do the likes of Dolce & Gabbana, Paul Smith, Chanel and Christian Dior. Many of these outlets are located in The Landmark (p.166), probably Hong Kong's best luxury shopping mall. Many of these designers (and countless others) can also be found in Harbour City (p.164) in TST or in and around Lee Gardens (p.167) in Causeway Bay. Prices are much the same as you would pay elsewhere in the world. Many other designer labels can be found in the larger malls, such as Pacific Place (p.167) or IFC Mall (p.164), while department stores Lane Crawford (p.172), Seibu (p.173) and Sogo (p.174) also stock a comprehensive range of designer wear at typically astronomical prices. Causeway Bay's trendy Paterson Street (map p.295, D-3) is also awash with hip international and local labels. For something with more of an eastern flavour, Shanghai Tang (2525 7333) in Central is the last word in Chinoise chic.

Computers

As with most electronic equipment, good places to start when looking for computers are the two main chains, Fortress (www.fortress.com.hk) and Broadway (www.broadway.com.hk). If you're in the market for an Apple Mac, however, try one of the branches of Ultimate PC & Mac Gallery (2899 2239), a reliable store with informed staff. Floors 11 and 12 of Windsor House in Causeway Bay (map p.295, E-3) are dedicated to computers and offer a range of PC and Mac retailers selling new and used machines, as well as a huge selection of accessories, cables, software and upgrades. For an unrivalled selection of computers and related products, Wan Chai is the easiest and best option. Two large multi-level shopping centres dedicated to computers sit across the road from each other beside the Hennessey Road exit of Wan Chai MTR station (map p.299, F-1). Wan Chai Computer Centre and 298 Computer Zone have literally thousands of new and used laptops, computers and games consoles for sale. Make sure to enquire about the extent of any warranty: many will only cover Hong Kong and not international repairs.

Jewellery, Watches & Gold

Hong Kong is a good place to buy pearl and jade jewellery – jade is an important, spiritual stone for the Chinese. Try the Jade Market in Yau Ma Tei (open 10:00-17:00, map p.304, B-1). You won't find high quality stones here, but it's a fascinating local experience and a great place to buy gifts. Bargaining is expected, and you should beware of fakes. For a more reliable place to shop for jade, Saturn Essentials is a lovely little shop off the cobbled steps of Pottinger Street in Central (map p.291, E-2). Another reasonably priced shop selling silver jewellery for men and women is Silver Ware at 537 Jaffe Road in Causeway Bay (map p.294, C-3).

For top of the line, exquisite pearls, head to Mikimoto in IFC Mall and Harbour City (both p.164), Cartier in the Prince's Building (p.168), or Chow Tai Fook (www.chowtaifook.com) with branches throughout Hong Kong.

Nathan Road in Mong Kok has a mind-boggling range of jewellers and watch shops. Take exit C1 when coming out of Mong Kok MTR station and peruse the shops either side of Argyle Road. Also on Kowloon side, in Hung Hom, is 3-D Gold Store (2766 3332), a giant jewellery shop famous for its luxury bathroom complete with solid gold toilets!

Perfumes & Cosmetics

Hong Kong being tax free on all but alcohol makes it the perfect place to buy perfume and cosmetics. Department Stores, such as Lane Crawford (p.172) and Sogo (p.174), have all the usual counters – Clarins, Estee Lauder, Aveda, Clinique and Christian Dior, to name a few. Some of these brands also have their own dedicated shops – the IFC Mall (p.164) is a good place to start as they stock a good variety. For less mainstream high-end brands, head to local fashion emporium Joyce (found in IFC Mall and Pacific Place) or Harvey Nichols (p.170). They have Chantecaille make-up, L'Artisan perfumes, and so on. Fairly new to Hong Kong is Australian skincare concept Aesop. At their signature shop on Lyndhurst Terrace (map p.291, D-3), they can mix up just the right product with a variety of aromatherapy oils and plant extracts.

Shoes

Hong Kong has an amazing selection of shoes from drop-dead $7,000 Jimmy Choo stilettos to cute $200 purple suede flats. On Pedder, which is located unsurprisingly on Pedder Street (map p.291, E-3), and Sergio Rossi next door are a treasure chest of luxury shoes. Department stores Lane Crawford (p.172), Seibu (p.173) and Sogo (p.174) also have a wide range of upmarket shoes, and because many are imported from Europe, they have at least some styles in sizes up to a UK eight. The Landmark (p.166) is a good mall to head to for designer shoe shops. Very cheap shoes of varying quality can be found in Hong Kong's markets (p.176).

Unfortunately, Asian-made shoes, which tend to come with a lower price tag, usually only go up to size 38 or sometimes 39 (UK size five or six), so for ladies with large feet, finding shoes can be frustrating. The same goes for men's shoes – many stores simply do not stock shoes above a UK size 10. For trainers, look no further than the area of Fa Yuen

Street known as 'Trainers Street' (map p.306, C-2). Almost every store in this area, including many of the smaller streets that branch off from Fa Yuen Street, are devoted to footwear. You will find a range of brands and styles that puts the majority of sports shops to shame, and prices are a good deal lower than you will pay elsewhere.

Souvenirs

Hong Kong is a great place to pick up souvenirs. There's a plethora of options – from fun $50 Mao watches and plastic models of the HSBC building to beautiful Chinese calligraphy scrolls and lacquerware. Markets (p.176) are always a good place to start. You can pick up anything from a pair of pretty embroidered Chinese ladies' slippers for $20, adorable childrens' outfits for $50 and statues of Hong Kong's favourite goddess, Kwun Yam. Stanley Market has a variety of stalls selling souvenirs, and also art shops selling works by local and regional artists. Some of the shops also have calligraphers on hand to paint your (or a family member's) name in Chinese for a small fee – these make fun gifts.

The chain of Chinese Arts and Crafts shops have a fantastic range of Chinese goods – jewellery, carvings, silk clothing, cushion covers, tableware and tea sets. There's a branch in Pacific Place (p.167). Shanghai Tang (2525 7333) also has lovely souvenirs and gifts with a designer touch – silver chopsticks, plush photo albums, handbags, baby booties embroidered with the Chinese characters for left and right, and their signature air spray that scents the shop in sweet frangipani hues.

Going Out

Hip Hong Kong

However much you're looking to spend, (or not to spend), whoever you want to be seen with, Hong Kong has a club, bar, restaurant or pub that's perfect.

Hong Kong offers world-class nightlife on a gleaming platter. Here you can find some of the best food, the swankiest bars and the hippest clubs in the world. And because variety is the spice of life, there are also plenty of earthier venues for those who like their nightlife gritty.

The range of restaurant styles and cuisines available is mind-boggling. You can eat in cheap and cheerful streetside stalls, in spectacular fine dining establishments, and everything in between. Chinese, Thai, French and Italian are among the most popular cuisines here, but you can also try Korean food, South African food, Scandinavian food and much more.

Many of Hong Kong's restaurants, bars and clubs are found in the following areas – Knutsford Terrace in Tsim Sha Tsui (map p.303 D-1), Lan Kwai Fong and SoHo in Central (map p.291 D-3 & E-3), and the infamous Wan Chai (map p.293 F-4).

Bars start to fill up after work at around 18:00, but things don't really get going until late. It's not unusual to have dinner at 21:00 and hit the bars after that. Then you can party all night.

This Going Out chapter is divided by area. The first page of each area has a handy Venue Finder, allowing you to see at a glance the various establishments on offer. The venue reviews then follow, with write-ups of the best restaurants, cafes, bars, pubs and clubs.

Blue Bar

Local Cuisine

The local cuisine is Cantonese and most food is steamed or stir-fried. The emphasis is on fresh ingredients. Vegetables are bought from the market daily and meat is often freshly slaughtered, with no body part wasted. The dishes are usually lightly flavoured with ginger, garlic, spring onions and soy sauce. Bean paste and chilli are used as dipping sauces.

A popular Cantonese speciality that you mustn't miss is Yum Cha (literally 'drink tea'). There are numerous tea houses and restaurants serving a variety of Chinese teas along with Dim Sum. These are small steamed or fried snacks often served in bamboo steamers stacked one on top of the other. You choose the dishes you want to eat, and at the end of the meal the empty steamers are counted and you are charged

accordingly. Although Yum Cha is usually a lunchtime occasion you can find restaurants serving Dim Sum through the night. It's a great way to sample Cantonese food and culture and is very reasonably priced.

Other styles of Chinese food are also well represented in Hong Kong, such as Szechuanese (hot and spicy), northern Chinese (wheat noodles, bread and mutton) and eastern Chinese (a mish mash of styles).

Vegetarian Food

Chinese cuisine relies heavily on meat, fish and seafood but there are many delicious vegetarian friendly dishes. Check out any Buddhist Chinese restaurant for vegan options. Many Indian restaurants also have a great choice of vegetarian cuisine. If you want western food and can't face another cheese omelette, try the Bookworm Café on Lamma Island (2982 4838), or Life in SoHo (p.231) for great organic vegetarian cooking. For Japanese vegetarian food try the Fortune vegetarian restaurant on Leighton Road, Causeway Bay (2881 1697). For an exhaustive list of veggie restaurants go to www.ivu.org/hkvegan/gb/hkrest.html.

Drinks

You must be at least 18 years of age to drink alcohol in Hong Kong. Other than that there are no rules. Alcohol is available everywhere – in corner shops, supermarkets and bottle shops, on ferries, in bars, restaurants, pubs and clubs. Bars, especially in popular areas, charge elevated prices for booze in order to cover elevated rents. Soft drinks are also expensive in restaurants and bars, and that includes water. You can try asking for tap water but some places have a no tap water 'policy'. Please feel free to kick up a stink.

Tax & Service Charges

Most restaurants will add a 10% service charge on top of the cost of the meal. If there is a service charge you will see it written at the bottom of the menu. If you eat out during Chinese New Year you may find a couple percent more added to the total to cover the extra staff costs. Otherwise there are no hidden surprises when you ask for the bill.

Tipping

Tipping is customary in most restaurants with waiting staff, with anything from 5-15% being the norm. The general practice is that any cash tips are pooled together and shared at the end of the night or week. Credit card tips are shared at the end of the month and companies quite often skim a little off the top. If you want to tip an individual server for good service, put the money in their hand and say, 'this is for you.'

The Yellow Star

This pretty yellow star is our way of highlighting places that we think merit extra praise. It could be the atmosphere, the food, the cocktails, the music or the crowd – but whatever the reason, any review that you see with the star attached is somewhere that we think is a bit special.

Venue Directory

Causeway Bay & Happy Valley

It's not all about the shopping and horse-racing – Causeway Bay & Happy Valley also make a great destination for a fun night out.

Causeway Bay is probably best known for its range of shopping options. The major malls and retail centres all have their own food outlets, often with fare a cut above the foodcourt burgers and pizzas you may expect. There's also a good selection of independent restaurants at this end of town, where hungry shoppers can refuel, rest their weary feet and give their credit cards a rest.

And if luck was on your side at the races, you may want to celebrate with a slap up meal. Amigo is recommended if you're determined to treat yourself. It's worth bearing in mind that if you visit this area on a race night, you'll be sharing the eating and drinking options (not to mention the taxis and MTR) with thousands of race-goers.

Venue Finder

Alfred's Grille	American	p.199
Inn Side Out	American	p.200
Dim Sum	Chinese	p.199
Watermargin	Chinese	p.200
Amigo	French	p.199
Sorabol	Korean	p.200

Restaurants

Alfred's Grille
American

15 Yuen Yuen St
2575 1322

Although the menu proclaims itself American, 'European' might be nearer the mark, featuring ingredients such as foie gras and Scottish salmon. The grill sees a lot of action, with meat, fish and vegetables all flamed to perfection. Muted tones and simple lines create an understated decor, though the small tables are a little close together. Map p.301 D4 **1**

Amigo
French

Amigo Mansion, 79A Wong Nai Chung Rd
2577 2202

At 40 years old, Amigo is an institution in Hong Kong. Waiters in black-tie uncover silver dishes from heated trolleys, the wine list is strictly Old World and the food is seriously good. The restaurant is located in a white-washed Spanish style villa and the surroundings match the food perfectly. It's not cheap, but there are lunch deals available. Map p.301 D3 **2**

Dim Sum
Chinese

63 Sing Woo Rd
2834 8893

Tastefully decorated with cream walls, dark wood furnishings and 50s advertising posters, this is one of Hong Kong's best dim sum restaurants. The menu has picture aids for the hard of Cantonese, but you can't go wrong with the dim sum. Many dishes come topped with shark's fin so be sure to specify 'no shark's fin' if you're concerned about this controversial practice. Map p.301 D4 **3**

Inn Side Out

American

Sunning Plaza, 10 Hysan Ave

2895 2900

In the alfresco dining area of this American-style restaurant and bar, palm trees tower over the tables while patrons munch on peanuts and toss the shells on the floor. The bar offers an extensive beer selection, and the all American food arrives in generous portions. Alongside the pizzas, pastas, burgers and sandwiches, the menu has a whole section dedicated to sausages. Bang on. 🚇 Causeway Bay, Map p.301 D1 **4**

Sorabol

Korean

Lee Theatre Plaza, 99 Percival St

2881 6823

Despite the strictly functional space, this Korean restaurant serves authentic, tasty food. Each table features a small grill for cooking your own food. The set menus include marinated meats to throw on the grill, a couple of Korean specialities and side dishes. You're bound to have fun here, but be prepared to leave wearing eau de bbq! 🚇 Causeway Bay, Map p.294 C4 **5**

Watermargin

Chinese

Times Square

3102 0088

Watermargin's apothecary drawers, red lanterns and antique woodcarvings exude the magic of old Northern China. The atmosphere is hip but welcoming, and staff will explain the dishes or suggest combinations. The food is occasionally spicy, and is best washed down with one of the recommended signature drinks. Each dish is beautifully arranged and the standard is high.

🚇 Causeway Bay, Map p.294 C4 **6**

Times Square, Causeway Bay

Central

With so many venues, Central lives up to its name as the centre of a great night out.

Venue Finder

Restaurants

Beirut
Arabic/Lebanese

Winner Bld, 27-37 D'Aguilar St
2804 6611

Beirut is one of the few Lebanese restaurants in Hong Kong. The entrance is on Lan Kwai Fong, where the ground floor is taken up almost entirely by the bar. The decor has a Middle Eastern theme, with orange and green tiles and minaret-shaped plastering. Most visitors drink or suck on shishas instead of sample the mezze menu. Upstairs, however, is a different realm. Rich materials and lanterns create a calmer, more exotic atmosphere where diners linger over light offerings such as hummus, tabouleh and lamb shawarma. Vegetarians in particular fare better here than in many of Hong Kong's eateries. 🔊 Central, Map p.291 E3 **7**

Bo Innovation
Fine Dining

U G/F, Ice House, 32-38 Ice House St
2850 8371

This restaurant has promptly earned a hot reputation among food cognoscenti. The cuisine is innovative Chino-Japanese, including bold but triumphant pairings, such as cucumber jelly and pumpkin rice pudding. Portion sizes are bang on and the bouji bar at one end of the restaurant offers a tantalising wine list. Dim lighting and gentle contemporary sounds create a cosy ambiance. The modish decor includes glass, dark stone and walnut. Expert staff will gladly guide diners through the menu. Here lies the undiscovered Hong Kong grail of eating establishments. 🔊 Central, Map p.291 E3 **8**

Cafe des Artistes
French
California Tower, 30-32 D'Aguilar St
2526 3880

With its wooden floors, pristine white tablecloths and chairs upholstered in muted tones, Cafe des Artistes looks like a smart French bistro. The comprehensive menu features all the classics, including endive salad, lobster bisque, and warm goat's cheese. Everything is tasty and beautifully presented and there is a good selection of French wines. The first floor location above Lan Kwai Fong makes this a great place for people watching. 🚇 Central, Map p.291 E3 **9**

Café Too
International
Island Shangri-La
2877 3838

Don't bother looking at the menu in this coffee shop-style restaurant – everyone's here for the fantastic value buffet ($258 Monday to Saturday, and $298 on Sundays). For that reason it's always packed, so bookings are essential. With seven different kitchens headed by 30 chefs, you'll find it difficult to choose between Japanese, Indian, Chinese and western cuisine. Don't miss the dessert station either, where you can dip squidgy marshmallows into a flowing chocolate fountain. Bring friends and an appetite. 🚇 Admiralty, Map p.298 B1 **10**

Caprice
Fine Dining
Four Seasons
3196 8888

Caprice sets out to deal in superlatives and delivers on every count. Think deep velvet seats, plush carpets, glittering chandeliers, cut glass and gilt-edged crockery. The waiting staff are extremely knowledgeable, without a hint of snobbery. However, Caprice's real triumph lies in the food. From the homely bread basket, the foie gras, the lamb with sage jus, through to the best cheese plate in town, this is contemporary French cuisine at its best. Naturally the wine list is monumental and there is a friendly sommelier to guide you through it. 🚇 Central, Map p.291 E1 **11**

Chez Moi
French
Arbuthnot House, 10 Arbuthnot Rd
2801 6768

As the name suggests, Chez Moi has such a welcoming interior it feels like you're in someone's much-loved front room. Quaint ornaments decorate shelves, leather armchairs sit by the window and a rocking chair wobbles by the reception desk. Each table is scattered with rose petals, making it popular with romantic Romeos. The menu boasts typical high-calibre French fare, including escargots, foie gras and veal chop – the chef's speciality.
🚇 Central, Map p.291 D3 **12**

China Tee Club
International
Pedder Bld, 12 Pedder St
2521 0233

A firm favourite of ladies who lunch, the twee China Tee Club instantly transports one back to yesteryear. Potted palms, ceiling fans, Edwardian furniture and little songbirds dotted about make for a tranquil oasis. Whether you prefer scones and clotted cream or dim sum, this is one of the best places in town for afternoon tea. Closes at 20:00.
🚇 Central, Map p.291 E3 **13**

Caprice

City Hall Maxim's Palace
City Hall, 5 Edinburgh Place

Chinese
2521 1303

Deservedly one of the most popular places in town to eat dim sum, you'll need to arrive early to avoid the queues. The steamed or fried snacks are served 50s style from passing trolleys pushed by old ladies, who'll happily show you each basket's contents if you can't read Chinese. Maxim's Palace offers not only tasty food and superb harbour views, but an authentic cultural experience - the noise, the frenzied service and the nagging suspicion you've just wolfed down a steaming bowl of pig's tripe and loved it. 📍 Central, Map p.292 A2 🎴

Dot Cod
Prince's Bld, 10 Chater Rd

Seafood
2810 6988

If you enjoy seafood, Dot Cod is the place for you – everything except the desserts involves the sea. This surprisingly spacious restaurant is located in the basement of Prince's building. Wander through the party atmosphere of the bar, which looks like a 1950s cruise ship, to the dining area with its art deco light fixtures and cast iron sculptures. Here, a mixed clientele enjoy elegant, but relaxed dining.
📍 Central, Map p.291 F3 🎴

Finds
Lan Kwai Fong Tower, Wyndham St

European
2522 9318

Finds takes its name from the five countries whose cuisine it represents – Finland, Iceland, Norway, Denmark and Sweden. The innovative dishes both look and taste like masterpieces. The large, airy space has a separate bar area which gets buzzy by early evening. Dining tables are well-spaced, and there's also al fresco seating available. The whole establishment is awash in shades of white and cool blue, lending an icy Nordic atmosphere.

Central, Map p.291 E3 **16**

Gaia
Italian

Grand Millenium Plaza, 181 Queen's Rd
2167 8200

Gaia is just off the beaten track in Sheung Wan. A welcoming, red lounge area to the left of the entrance is ideal for an aperitif. The main dining room has floor-to-ceiling windows and large sliding doors leading onto the terrace. The food has the freshest imported ingredients and there are a fine selection of pastas, thin-crust pizzas and fuller mains. An extensive wine list is also available - ask the Maitre d' for recommendations. Gaia attracts its fair share of celebrities, and no wonder, it's the best Italian in town.

Sheung Wan, Map p.291 D1 **17**

Good Luck Thai
Thai

13 Wing Wah Lane
2877 2971

Affectionately known as 'Rat Alley' among expats, Wing Wah Lane is an HK institution. Many an arduous night in LKF's bars begins in its restaurants, including Good Luck Thai. Staples such as tom yum goong, pomelo salads and curries of various hues abound. Washed down with chilled beer, everything is cheap and tasty, and the atmosphere is very relaxed. While here, look out for the infamous Indian Elvis.

Central, Map p.291 E3 **7**

Habibi Cafe
Arabic/Lebanese

112-114 Wellington St
2544 3886

This fantastic Egyptian-owned eatery is as close as you'll get to ancient Cairo in modish Hong Kong. You'll find old Arab films playing above the bar and photographs of Cairo's vanished 'beau monde'. The food is irreproachable, including mezze, grilled meats and bowls of the koshary street-staple. Try the excellent value 'Mediterranean Magic' mezze combo with a glass of iced kharkadee (hibiscus) tea. Round everything off with home-made sweets or an apple-flavoured shisha. Divine. 🔊 Central, Map p.291 D2 **19**

Harvester
Vegetarian

Yardley Commercial Bld, New Market St
2542 4788

One of Hong Kong's few true vegetarian restaurants, this is pretty basic – think fold away tables, plastic plates and paper napkins. However, it's also tasty and cheap as chips. Food is served buffet style – you help yourself to rice, soup, and a small selection of main dishes, and your meal is then weighed and you are charged accordingly. The dishes change every day but it's all Canto style veggie food with a large emphasis on tofu. 🔊 Sheung Wan, Map p.290 C1 **20**

Indochine 1929
Vietnamese

California Tower
2869 7399

For authentic Vietnamese cuisine, this place is hard to beat. In the hub of Lan Kwai Fong, IndoChine oozes French Colonial charm. Well established for the area (1993), it has a loyal clientele so booking is advised. The beef tenderloin with tomatoes, braised duck with orange sauce, and Hanoi style fish all come recommended, and regulars swear by the black sticky rice with red bean, coconut milk and roasted peanuts. Definitely worth blowing the budget for.

Central, Map p.291 E3 9

Isola
Italian
IFC Mall
2383 8765

In a packed city, Isola is space and light. Flanked by the harbour, the restaurant is divided between an all-white interior, a broad patio for outdoor dining and a leafy roof-top bar offering spectacular views of the city. The food, created by Italian chef Gianni Caprioli, is fresh and wide-ranging, and each dish is beautifully presented. For atmospheric fine dining by the harbour, Isola is hard to beat.

Central, Map p.291 F1 22

Jim Chai Kee Noodles
Chinese
Jade Ctr, 98 Wellington St
2850 6471

Jim Chai Kee was recently renovated for the better. Gone are the chipped formica table tops and plastic stools. Now modern, wood-veneered tables and benches are crammed with diners enjoying one of the three dishes on the menu: prawn wonton, beef or fish ball noodles. Expect to queue, to be served within minutes and turfed out as soon as you've finished. However, for the price you won't find a better meal in HK and the management know it.

Central, Map p.291 E2 23

Kyoto Joe
Japanese
The Plaza, 21 D'Aguilar St
2804 6800

Kyoto Joe offers contemporary Japanese cuisine at realistic prices. The upper floor features a laid-back sake bar and a robatayaki counter where you can watch the chefs cooking up a storm. Downstairs, dark-wood furnishings and vertical plasma screens blend traditional and modern decor. The menu is wide ranging and runs the gamut of Japanese cuisine – the sushi, seared tuna and seabass dishes are particularly recommended. 🔲 Central, Map p.291 E3 **7**

Le Parisien
French
IFC Mall
2805 5293

Le Parisien is wonderfully located with a phenomenal harbour view. The design is clean and modern with wood panelling and windows the length of the restaurant. Dishes of note include the traditional canard au sang, and the rustic crispy pig's trotter galette. For the less adventurous, there's a broad choice of more mainstream dishes on offer. The wine selection is extensive and very well-chosen. Open for dinner and lunch, this is a pleasantly unstuffy restaurant of supreme quality that lets the food speak for itself.

🔲 Central, Map p.291 F1 **22**

Lot 10
Mediterranean
34 Gough St
2813 6812

Lot 10 is situated in NoHo – an up-and-coming area hoping to rival SoHo. The restaurant has a seaside villa feel, and features a tiny downstairs dining area and a slightly larger room and terrace upstairs. The theme is Mediterranean, with wooden benches, blue and white furnishings and soft amber lights. The French and Italian menu includes delicacies such as pan-fried foie gras and a tasty pasta and risotto section. Look out for the homemade chocolate cake which is just divine.

⊞ Central, Map p.291 D2 26

Lumiere/Cuisine Cuisine

IFC Mall

Chinese
2393 3933

The experience justifies the cost in this phenomenal Chinese restaurant. The high-ceilinged space is separated into both a Szechuanese bistro and a more formal Cantonese restaurant, while Hong Kong harbour views are complemented by a beautiful bronze and blonde wood decor. Here, traditional Chinese food is transformed into haute cuisine. The seafood is delivered fresh daily and they make their own soy sauces (crucial for good Chinese food).

⊞ Central, Map p.291 F1 22

Lung King Heen

Four Seasons

Chinese
3196 8888

This top-class Chinese eatery is one of the most stylish and contemporary in town. With its rich brown wooden walls and floor, dark wood tables and brushed steel ceiling, it's a chic blend of old and new, and the view across the harbour to Kowloon waterfront makes a spectacular backdrop for a spectacular meal. It has a vast menu, featuring traditional delicacies, such as bird's nest soup, as well as modern seafood dishes and desserts. ⊞ Central, Map p.291 E1 11

M at the Fringe

Fringe Club, 2 Lower Albert Rd

European

2877 4000

This small venue, a survivor in Hong Kong's fickle restaurant scene, has a romantic feel with earthy orange and green walls, low lighting and a huge central floral bouquet. The food has influences from all over Europe, Turkey, Morocco and Lebanon. Ingredients are wonderfully fresh and those with a sweet tooth will love the Grand Dessert – a sample platter featuring six desserts, including the legendary M pavlova.

🚇 Central, Map p.291 E3 **29**

NoHo Cafe

24 Gough St

International

2813 2572

In Hong Kong's only bed cafe, the bunks are lined up along one side of the restaurant and are intimately sealed off by silk curtains. It's fabulous for a date, and if you really want to get close there's a sealed-off VIP bed chamber complete with TV and a wide selection of films. The food comes from around the globe with enticing appetizers such as meaty oven-baked mussels with crispy bacon in crumbly filo pastry.

🚇 Sheung Wan, Map p.291 D2 **26**

Pierre

Mandarin Oriental

French

2522 0111

The menu here shows off fresh takes on classical French dishes, and changes regularly to focus on seasonal foods. The modern decor, dark colour scheme and rich textures provide a luxurious and intimate atmosphere, and the striking view of Victoria Harbour can be seen from all over the restaurant.

There's really no need to mention the prices – you probably already have an idea. ☺ Central, Map p.291 F3 **31**

Post 97

Lan Kwai Fong

International

2810 9333

Post 97 is a Hong Kong institution. People come here before a big night out in The Fong – or for breakfast following a big night in The Fong. It's hard to describe the bizarre decor: there's a lot of red, a few gold cupids and a bird's nest. The international dishes are tasty and there are even healthy options if you hope to atone for your sins.

☺ Central, Map p.291 E3 **9**

Song

75 Hollywood Rd

Vietnamese

2559 0997

Drop down a few steps into the quaint Man Hing Lane and you will find the hidden entrance to this small restaurant. A white colour scheme, billowing sheer drapes and candles galore make the restaurant feel like a spa. The modern take on Vietnamese cuisine sees a menu full of small, light dishes boasting expertly balanced flavours. The tables are few, conversations are hushed, and first time visitors will feel they've discovered a real hidden treasure.

☺ Central, Map p.291 D2 **33**

Thai Lemongrass

California Tower, 30-32 D'Aguilar

Thai

2905 1688

From the barman's green silk suit to the single malts and Cuban cigars he serves, Thai Lemongrass is immediately a step above many HK Thai eateries. For a decade the restaurant has served inspired, varied Thai dishes to couples and businessmen. It excels in seafood, such as deep-fried sea bass with tamarind and chilli, and a range of curries, including roast duck in red curry with grapes and aubergines. Flavours are delicately balanced and dishes feel light. 🔲 Central, Map p.291 E3 **9**

TRU
Fusion

Grand Progress Bld
2525 6700

The food here is modern Thai-Vietnamese fusion, and this is reflected in the tasteful decor. The menu is short but well thought out, offering fresh takes on traditional dishes, and an open kitchen allows you to watch your food being created. Vegetarians are well catered for and everything is beautifully presented. There is a good wine list as well as some interesting cocktails, and prices are very reasonable for the area. 🔲 Central, Map p.291 E3 **9**

Veda
Indian

8 Arbuthnot Rd
2868 5885

Often crowned Hong Kong's top Indian restaurant, Veda offers contemporary twists on regional cuisine. The interior is harmoniously decorated in neutral chrome with mirrored mosaic designs. Food is expertly prepared and the open kitchen allows you to spy on the process. The curries with aromatic spices are unusually zesty. There's also an eclectic wine list with new and old world offerings. If you find the price tag high, try the value lunch menu for $108.

🔲 Central, Map p.291 D4 **16**

Yung Kee Restaurant

Chinese

32-40 Wellington St

2522 1624

This award-winning restaurant first opened its doors in 1942 – so it's practically ancient in Hong Kong years. It's since expanded its premises and menu, although the roast goose remains the house speciality. You can dine on any of the three opulently decorated upper floors, or opt for the more boisterous ground floor. Expect to see a huge hungry clientele, including secretaries, A-listers and tourists.

🚇 Central, Map p.291 E3 **37**

Bars & Pubs

Al's Diner

Bar

39 D'Aguilar St

2521 8714

Every night is party night at Al's. It's bursting on Fridays and Saturdays with revellers happily spilling out onto the streets of Lan Kwai Fong, suffering from lessening control over their limbs and moderate hearing loss. Eighties tunes scream out of giant video screens while the thirty-something crowd gyrate on tables. By contrast Al's is quiet during the day, and a great place to enjoy some of the best burgers and shakes in town. 🚇 Central, Map p.291 E3 **7**

Bit Point

Bar

31 D'Aguilar St

2523 7436

Uncompromisingly German, this bar serves some of the finest beers in Hong Kong as well as a great selection of schnapps. The snack platter includes sausages, cold cuts, cheese &

gherkins. If you want a more substantial meal you can order a hearty German classic such as meatloaf. Functionally designed with plain wooden tables and cosy booths, Bit Point is dominated by a long bar where patrons sit to drink and chat with the warm and welcoming bar staff.

Central, Map p.291 E3 **7**

Blue Bar
Four Seasons

Bar
3196 8888

If this place were a car, it would be a Ferrari – slick, expensive and popular with the rich and power hungry. The aerodynamic leather chairs are softened by velvet cushions, a lit column of glass throws shades of blue across the room and plush carpeting softens the click, click of designer heels. There's a long list of cocktails as well as fine wines and champagnes, and a cigar menu featuring top of the range smokes. Needless to say, none of this comes cheap, but that's probably part of the appeal. Central, Map p.291 E1 **11**

The Cavern
55 D'Aguilar St

Bar
2121 8969

Decorated in homage to the Swinging Sixties, with shag pile walls and psychedelic flourishes, The Cavern is best known for its live music, which is usually provided by tribute bands honouring rock'n'roll's greatest names. Go with a large group and you're bound to have some good, tacky fun. The menu is limited, but the dishes are tasty, well presented and more imaginative than in similar bars. Central, Map p.291 E3 **16**

Club 97

Bar

9 Lan Kwai Fong   2186 1897

Club 97 is a long-standing lynchpin of trendy Lan Kwai Fong. The classy decor includes plenty of marble and candles, and mirrored curtains frame the entrance giving a theatrical look. The menu is funky with drinks to match. The club hosts top-notch local and international DJs – if you like house, you'll find it by the bucket load here. There are also special nights featuring latin, reggae and funk. 🚇 Central, Map p.291 E3 **9**

Fringe Club

Bar

2 Lower Albert Rd   2521 7251

The relaxed rooftop bar makes a pleasant change from the more self conscious bars in the area and is also one of the few places in Central with plenty of outdoor seating. It's a pretty basic set up with aluminium tables and chairs dotted around on the Astroturf. Drinks are reasonably priced and there's a snack menu available, although offerings are mediocre at best. You may well catch an art or photography exhibition on display in the small, indoors part of the bar.
🚇 Central, Map p.291 E3 **29**

Gecko

Bar

Ezra Lane   2537 4680

Reached through a tiny lane opposite the hot dog stall underneath the Mid-Levels Escalator, this laid-back spot more than makes up for in atmosphere what it lacks in size. Comfy, cushion-scattered sofas line the walls below collections of paintings and photography by local artists, and the music policy is top notch, ranging from sexy French house to salsa beats. DJs perform at the weekends and Wednesday is live jazz night. There's a great wine list, and you shouldn't forget to try the absinthe. 🔊 Central, Map p.291 D3 **44**

The Globe
Pub

39 Hollywood Rd   2543 1941

This quintessentially British pub is renowned for its extensive selection of ales, both bottled and on tap, and a hearty bar menu. Live Premiership football draws the crowds on a Saturday, and the Tuesday night quiz is popular too. Music comes courtesy of one of the city's best-stocked jukeboxes, where even the most discerning of audiophiles should find something to their liking. The down side to The Globe is that it can get quite smoky. 🔊 Central, Map p.291 D3 **44**

Half Past Ten
Bar

10 Glenealy   2869 9089

As stylish as it is comfortable, Half Past Ten is a little-known gem in the Hong Kong bar scene. Located up the hill from the Fringe Club, its unassuming exterior gives way to a chic monochrome interior featuring low-slung tables and seats. The emphasis here is on chilling out, a fact reflected in the music policy, although the pace quickens somewhat at the weekend. Even when busy, Half Past Ten feels intimate thanks to the clever seating arrangement, which includes a secluded alcove. For those in the know, this is a popular spot for pre-club cocktails, and the martinis come highly recommended.

🔊 Central, Map p.291 E4 **45**

Hardy's Folk Club
Bar
35 D'Aguilar St
2526 7184
Hardy's is the black sheep of Lan Kawi Fong. The interior is grungy, with worn furniture, an exposed concrete ceiling and not much in the way of decor. Nevertheless, Hardy's is special. It caters to one of the most diverse crowds in Hong Kong and everyone is made to feel welcome. Come in black tie or a bin liner – nobody cares. Things really get going at about ten when karaoke kicks off, with singers accompanied by the talented resident guitarist. Reasonably priced beers and jello shots help ease the nerves. 🚇 Central, Map p.291 E3 **7**

La Dolce Vita
Bar
9 Lan Kwai Fong
2186 1888
La Dolce Vita is the doyenne of the Lan Kwai Fong open-fronted bar. There's often a large wine-drinking fiesta spilling onto the street outside. Inside, the look is modern, with lots of black, white and red. The snack menu offers all the usual suspects and the generous portions are all fresh and tasty. There's a small but well-chosen selection of wine and the monthly specials occasionally turn up some real treasures. Classic cocktails and enticing shooters keep people coming back. 🚇 Central, Map p.291 E3 **9**

Linq
Bar
35 Pottinger St
2971 0680
Linq is a cosy little bar off the cobbled Pottinger Street. It has a cellar feel to it with brick walls and hanging lanterns. Everyone here is very friendly, including the excellent bar

staff. Another plus is that single women don't need to worry about unwanted attention. The only oddity is the music which doesn't quite seem to match the crowd. A tiny booth houses the resident DJ who spins funky house. 🔊 Central, Map p.291 D3 **49**

Lotus
37-43 Pottinger St
Bar
2543 6290

The main draw at Lotus is the excellent Thai food, dished up by infamous Sydney chef and master of modern Asian cuisine, Will Meyrick. However plenty of young hipsters come here just to drink. There's a mean cocktail list with inventive martinis, belinis and bartenders who shake their thingies. The contemporary Asian design matches the menu with plenty of modern lattice screens and red leather seats.
🔊 Central, Map p.291 D3 **49**

MO Bar
The Landmark, Mandarin Oriental
Bar
2132 0077

Hong Kong has more than its fair share of swanky bars, but this one has the clout to out-glitz them all. During the day it's a haven for local fashionistas, tai tais and ladies who lunch. At night, the atmosphere turns sexy and seductive, with the giant 'O' that dominates one wall casting its warm red glow across the stylish furnishings. MO is large enough to accommodate the many style mavens, hotel guests and celebrities who descend here at weekends, and pricey enough to leave your wallet feeling considerably lighter after just one or two drinks. A smart-casual dress code is enforced.
🔊 Central, Map p.291 F3 **51**

Top: MO Bar. Bottom: Soda

Soda
Bar
79 Wyndham St   2522 8118

Soda is a colourful and well-designed spot in which to enjoy a drink or a bite at any time of the day or night. Retro furniture gives the bar a fun feel, while cool beats courtesy of in-house DJs enhance the relaxed vibe. There's an impressive wine list, and Soda is also known for its excellent cocktails. Should you get a sudden attack of the munchies, there's a menu of reasonably priced burgers, pizzas, sandwiches and the like.

Central, Map p.291 D3 **52**

Stormy Weather Bar & Grill
Bar
48 D'Aguilar St   2845 5533

Affectionately known as Stormies, this bar and restaurant at the top of Lan Kwai Fong starts to fill up early and is overflowing by the end of the night. There's a vaguely nautical theme inside, and drinks are also named in a nautical fashion. The emphasis is on seafood, with crabs a speciality, but salads, steaks and sandwiches are served too. Fans of 80s and 90s pop and rock will love this place. Stormies attracts a sociable crowd and you're bound to make new friends before the night is out.   Central, Map p.291 E3 **7**

Yumla
Bar
Harilela House, 79 Wyndham St   2147 2383

Yumla isn't so much a bar as a Hong Kong institution. In a city where many of the clubs are concerned with looking stylish and having exclusive door policies, this bar-cum-club is a glorious exception. Small in size but colossal in stature, Yumla has DJ nights every Friday and Saturday that sizzle through to the early hours, with playlists that boast an eclectic mix of sounds. Whether it be breakbeat, jungle, drum'n'bass or experimental electro, Yumla always has an up-for-it crowd and a superb atmosphere. 🚇 Central, Map p.291 D3 **52**

Nightclubs

Dragon-i
The Centrium, 60 Wyndham St

Nightclub
3110 1222

Dragon-i is the favourite hang out of models, actors and wannabes, and to get through the door you'd better be beautiful or look like you have wads of cash. Inside the lighting is moody and the decor glamorously modern – even the steel-doored unisex toilets are worth a visit. Dragon-i is all about show, and the champagne quaffing expat men and East European models certainly make quite a spectacle.

🚇 Central, Map p.291 D3 **12**

Drop
On Lok Mansion, 39-43 Hollywood Rd

Nightclub
2543 8856

This small club is wildly popular, mainly because of its legendary music policy. Any self respecting clubber visits Drop regularly to hear the best DJs in town. In fact it's so popular that the queues have become its main downfall. Once inside though, you'll find a pretty friendly crowd that gets more and more raucous as the night wears on. Drinks are suitably strong and the fresh fruit cocktails are delicious.

🚇 Central, Map p.291 D3 **44**

Hei Hei Club
Nightclub
1 On Hing Terrace
2899 2068

This 7,000 sq ft club is named after the Chinese character meaning double happiness. The decor has a Balinese resort feel to it, the highlights of which are the tiny pool and petal-strewn Jacuzzis on the terrace, and there is plenty of outdoor space. The music is a mix of hip hop and R&B. There are cocktails galore (with exotic prices), professional staff and plenty of beautiful people to look at. 🚇 Central, Map p.291 E3 57

Home
Nightclub
23 Hollywood Rd
2545 0023

Staying open until dawn and beyond, Home is the final stop for many people after a long, hard night on the tiles. Weary revellers opt for the large, Thai-style mattresses, divided by sheets of billowing white fabric. Here, you can flick off your shoes and recline in comfort with a bunch of your closest or newest friends. 🚇 Central, Map p.291 D3 58

Volar
Nightclub
38-44 D'Aguilar St
2810 1276

One of the hottest clubs in Hong Kong, Volar strikes a fine balance between style and substance. For those who enjoy chic surroundings, the futuristic labyrinthe interior hits the mark. Audiophiles, meanwhile, will revel in the club's top-notch sound system. The door policy is strict, so you generally need to be a member or on the guest list to get in. Drinks are expensive and strong, making the many rooms and corridors even harder to navigate. 🚇 Central, Map p.291 E3 7

Dragon-i

served within. With its authentic Szechuan cuisine, dim lighting and deep reddish walls, this place will send temperatures soaring during an intimate meal. However, there are plenty of options for those wanting to keep their taste buds unsinged. Service is superbly attentive, so you'll always have a cold beer on hand to douse the flames.

Central, Map p.291 D3 62

Craftsteak
Steakhouses
29 Elgin St
2526 0999

This is a steakhouse with a difference. Choose from steaks (Australian, Argentinian or Canadian), lamb, pork, poultry or seafood, then pick your favourite sauce and vegetable dish. The meat is then cooked over an open flame. The interior of the restaurant is done out in dark woods and creams. The kitchen is open to the restaurant so you can see the team at work. Be warned, however, the steaks here are so good you may never want anything else again. Central, Map p.291 D3 60

El Taco Loco
Mexican
9 Staunton St
2147 9000

Set right at the mouth of SoHo, this is a great place for a cheap and scrumptious meal, a couple of cheeky margaritas and some serious people watching. The menu is innovative and outlines a variety of different meat, fish and vegetable options which can be served in a number of different ways. The Carnitas (a deep fried pork burrito) comes highly recommended, but for the cholesterol conscious there are plenty of other goodies to choose from. Central, Map p.291 D3 64

La Comida

G/F 22 Staunton St

Spanish
2530 3118

La Comida is typical of SoHo restaurants in that it's small and intimate. Two rows of small tables with banquette seats run the length of the room. The warm colours of Spain feature heavily with yellow tableclothes, deep red cushions and orange walls. There's a long list of delicious tapas, along with four different paellas and the obligatory sangria, as well as some authentic dessert options. La Comida attracts a mixed crowd, and fills up quickly even at lunch time.

Central, Map p.291 D3 64

La Pampa

32 Staunton St

Argentina
2868 6959

It's all about the meat at this Argentinean restaurant. While the interior is simple and homely with pale yellow walls and caramel-coloured chairs, the menu is a carnivore's paradise. Steaks feature prominently, and the prices are reasonable, and portions generous. Other options include salads, native sausages and fish dishes. A reasonably priced bottle of Argentinean wine is the best way to wash down your meal.

Central, Map p.291 D3 64

Life

10 Shelly St

Vegetarian
2810 9777

This organic vegetarian restaurant has an extensive menu offering wholesome snacks and meals, revitalising juices and cleansing teas. Those with food intolerances and restricted diets are well catered to. The restaurant has a wholesome feel with natural tones and lots of wood. On the second floor, the small roof garden is a pleasant place to sit on cooler days. Its main drawback is the service which is at times painfully slow. 🏙 Central, Map p.291 D3 67

Nutmeg Grill
37 Elgin St

International
2522 3850

You'll either love or hate Nutmeg Grill's psychedelic purple and yellow interior with squidgy seating, groovy music and wavy patterns. As for the menu, it may be limited, but the food is fabulous. Tasty appetizers include freshly-caught steamed clams in white wine sauce and tuna served with buffalo mozzarella. For the main course, deliciously tender veal stuffed with parma ham and succulent pork loin chops both come highly recommended. 🏙 Central, Map p.291 D3 60

Olive
32 Elgin St

Fusion
2521 1608

Olive offers dishes from the Middle East and the Mediterranean, with main courses ranging from rabbit and leek pie to rich seafood tagines. There's a high quality wine list, and a dessert menu with treats like yoghurt and honey pannacotta with toffeed strawberries. The restaurant has an intimate feel with subdued lighting and dark wood interiors, and the staff can make informed, affordable recommendations. If you're here for romance, ask for one of the tucked-away tables. 🏙 Central, Map p.291 D3 60

Clockwise from top left: Bizou, La Pampa, Olive

Bars & Pubs

Feather Boa
Bar
38 Staunton St
2857 2586

An open secret for those in the know, Feather Boa harks back to a forgotten era of decadent Eastern European coffee bars and glamorous Parisian nightclubs. From the outside there are no signs to indicate Feather Boa's existence, but open the antique blue door and push through the heavy velvet curtains and another world awaits within. It's small and intimate, so arrive early to get a seat and relax with magical goblets of potent cocktails served by ethereal bartenders. 🚇 Central, Map p.291 D3 **64**

Joyce Is Not Here
Bar
38-44 Peel St
2851 2999

If you want to chill out while talking art, film, music or poetry with like-minded souls, then this is the place for you. One wall displays a smorgasbord of magazines, books, paintings, objets d'art and photographs. All are available to buy. Drinks include beers, spirits, alcohol-spiked coffees and house-speciality cocktails, while a thoughtfully created selection of snacks is also available. The bar has Wednesday night poetry readings, regular jam sessions, and films are shown on Sunday evenings. 🚇 Central, Map p.291 D3 **71**

McSorley's Ale House
Pub
55 Elgin St
2522 2646

With a traditional pub facade contrasting with the offices and apartments above, McSorley's is hard to miss.

Inside though, this Irish pub is refreshingly free of 'Oirish' memorabilia – there's not a picture of Yeats or old Dublin in sight. Instead there's an attractive wooden bar on each of its floors, serving a wide variety of whiskies and several ales, and, of course, Guinness. The menu is not for the light stomached. From fish and chips to burgers and pies, this is good, straight food for drinkers. ☐ Central, Map p.291 D3 60

Nzingha Lounge
48 Peel St

Bar
2834 6866

This bar is welcoming and cosy with an earthy feel. The low, mismatched chairs and tables are draped in rich African fabrics, and the walls are dotted with folk art. There's an unusual list of house cocktails, which are generally heavy on the rum as well as a small menu of authentic African nibbles. There's plenty of room to lounge, although most people come here to get down to the African beats proffered by the resident DJ. ☐ Central, Map p.291 D3 71

Staunton's Wine Bar and Cafe
10-12 Staunton St

Bar
2973 6611

Staunton's location next to the Escalator makes it a prime spot to grab a drink and spy on would-be-dates coming home from work. Chic and relaxed, it can nevertheless get frantic in the early evenings, with loyal patrons spilling onto the busy streets with their Happy Hour Sauvignon Blancs. By day though, you can grab a paper and relax with a cappuccino. If you're feeling peckish, they've got a great bistro menu. ☐ Central, Map p.291 D3 64

Alfresco eateries, fabulous seafood and unpretentious bars on the beach – escape from the high rises and pace of the city and see what the south of Hong Kong Island has to offer.

When you need a break from the non-stop city, the south of the Island has a host of relaxing options, and that goes for its restaurants and bars, too. Taking full advantage of the coastal location, many of the venues in this section enjoy stunning sea views, while some are so close you could dip your toes in the water between courses.

Venue Finder

Restaurants

The Blue Room   International
Big Wave Bay   2809 2583
Big Wave Bay is about as far as you can get without leaving
the island and the Blue Room is the last pit-stop before
plunging into the surf. This simple, beach-side cafe caters
equally well to surfers, expat families and flirting teenagers.
The 'Dawn Patrol' menu features everything from a full fry-up
to pancakes with strawberries. The lunchtime menu offers
salads, wraps, and pasta dishes. On weekends they serve a
surprisingly good thin crust pizza that goes perfectly with
their ice-cold beers. Map p.289 F3

The Boathouse   International
88 Stanley Main St   2813 4467
The Boathouse is arguably the best of the seafront
restaurants in Stanley and is usually packed to the gills. The
restaurant is spread over three floors, including a balcony and
roof top terrace. In fair weather the windows are flung open
making the place bright and airy. Known for its seafood, the
enormous seafood platter is excellent, as are the fresh, tangy
salads, overstuffed sandwiches, and delicious desserts.
Map p.289 E4

Chilli N Spice   International
Murray House, Stanley Plaza   2899 0147
This restaurant is located in Murray House, a grand stone
building first erected in Central in 1843, then dismantled and

rebuilt in Stanley a few years ago. Worth a visit for this reason alone, the restaurant itself is large and airy, while a balcony wraps itself around the restaurant and makes a very pleasant place to sit and gaze out to sea. The delicious and reasonably priced menu offers a host of Southeast Asian favourites such as Singaporean chilli crab and Indonesian chicken satay.

Map p.289 E4

Cococabana
Mediterranean
Beach Bld, Island Rd, Deep Water Bay
2812 2226

Simple but elegant, Cococabana is rapidly establishing itself as one of the top al fresco dining options in HK. Set right on the beach and commanding a view over the bay, white sofas and tables combine with candlelight to create an irresistibly romantic mood. The owner, Jean Paul Gaucci, ensures the consistently delicious rotating menu has a Mediterranean twist, with norms such as foie gras, lamb tagine with couscous, or fresh tomato salad. Map p.289 D3

El Cid
Spanish
Murray House, Stanley Plaza
2899 0858

This Spanish restaurant is mercifully free of sombreros and pictures of flamenco dancers. Instead, the restaurant is understated with wood panelled walls, black and white checked marble floors and large wooden shutters. A balcony wraps around the restaurant and provides most of the restaurant's space, plus a pleasant view out to sea. The menu features the usual favourites, including seafood paella and a selection of tapas. Map p.289 E4

Lucy's

64 Stanley Main St

Mediterranean

2813 9055

This small restaurant has no windows, but it's cosy rather than claustrophobic. Decor is Mediterranean-inspired with warm orange walls and splashes of yellow and green. The perfect break from the tourist circuit, Lucy's offers a daily set menu – a bargain at $158 for three courses – or you can opt for a la carte. The menu is short but tempting, offering innovative takes on traditional Mediterranean fare. Map p.289 E4

Shek O Chinese and Thailand Seafood Restaurant

303 Shek O Village

Thai

2809 2202

This restaurant is a stone's throw from the beach and a favourite with beachgoers and hikers braving routes along the Dragon's Back. It would be totally outdoors were it not for a smattering of concrete overhead, a bit of tin and some awning. Folding tables, a murky fish tank, and an ultra laid back atmosphere set the scene. Nevertheless, cheery weekend diners wolf down the standard Thai food with gusto, then marvel at the modest bill. Map p.289 F3

Spices

109 Repulse Bay Rd

Asian Subcontinent

2292 2821

Maintaining the colonial feel of the building that houses it, the interior is elegant with high ceilings and lots of dark wood. However, the real draw is the large terrace where round tables look out over the bay. The menu offers a range of dishes from South East Asia, and most customers end up sharing. The lengthy drinks list boasts fresh juices and cocktails. Everything on the menu is tasty, attractively presented and reasonably priced. Map p.289 D3

Bars & Pubs

Back Beach Bar
Bar

Back Beach, Shek O

This place is little more than a hole in the wall with a few tables on the walkway above the beach. But what it lacks in style, it makes up for in atmosphere. On a sunny Saturday afternoon, a chilled out crowd leans back and sips cheap beers whilst dogs and toddlers run around freely. In the evening, groups merge and parties often appear from nowhere. Don't be surprised if someone pulls out a guitar and starts strumming a tune. Map p.289 F3

The Smugglers Inn
Pub

90A Stanley Main St
2813 8852

One of the oldest and possibly most authentic English pubs in Hong Kong, this relaxed and friendly bar comes complete with dark wooden beams across the ceiling and furniture made from old barrels. Don't expect fancy cocktails. This is a beer, darts and juke box establishment. They serve a mean ploughman's too. The Smuggler's Inn fills up alarmingly early in the day and is a great place to sip a cold beer and gaze across the bay. Map p.289 E4

VODKA NIGHT
8:00 PM - 10:00 PM
EVERY FRIDAY

Tsim Sha Tsui

A host of swanky venues can be found in TST's top hotels, and Knutsford Terrace offers a wide choice of restaurants and bars to while away an evening.

With its vast selection of top-notch venues, Tsim Sha Tsui gives Central a run for its money in the going out stakes. It's got swanky bars with spectacular views, high class restaurants with prices to match, and even the obligatory Irish pub.

Venue Finder

Restaurants

Balalaika
Russian

10 Knutsford Terrace
2312 6222

The hearty food, folk art, and large tables give this place
a Russian peasant feel. The piroshki (dumplings), shashlik
(kebab) and caviar provide a good foundation for a walk into
the frozen vodka room. Don a fur coat and down a range
of vodka shots at -20 degrees centigrade. On most nights
there's live Russian folk music and yes, the balalaika regularly
appears. As you can imagine, the crowd gets rowdy as the
evening rolls on. 🚇 Tsim Sha Tsui, Map p.303 D1 75

Gaddi's
Fine Dining

The Peninsula Hong Kong
2315 3171

Gaddi's caters to a slightly older crowd. One who appreciates
the blue and golden hued decor, the grovelling service and
above all, the fine French cuisine – all the ingredients are
imported from France, even the lemons. Most dishes are
traditional, hearty fair, with a few lighter options available.
The marinated goose liver, lobster bisque and Bresse pigeon
are all recommended. Needless to say, there is a suitably
lengthy list of wines and a sommelier to guide you through it.
🚇 Tsim Sha Tsui, Map p.302 C4 76

Hibiki
Japanese

Knutsford Terrace, Kimberley Plaza
2316 2884

Along with its tasteful combination of classical and
contemporary Japanese cuisine, Hibiki elegantly serves over 100

types of sake. The food menu features the standard selection of tempura, sushi and sashimi as well as innovative selections like goose liver and mango sushi. Meat options include lamb chops with plum miso or duck breast wit hot apple sauce. Top it off with Japanese ice creams and sherbets. The clean lines and minimalist furnishings are very Japanese and the atmosphere is friendly and relaxed. 🚇 Tsim Sha Tsui, Map p.303 D1 **77**

Hoi King Heen
InterContinental Grand Stanford

Chinese
2731 2882

The Cantonese fare at Hoi King Heen is interpreted in a lighter, less oily way with unusual ingredients such as asparagus and pine nuts. The result is delicious. Décor is typical hotel style – cherry wood round tables cater to small groups and couples, while private rooms accommodate larger parties. Diners can watch the chefs at work in the glass-walled kitchen and a specialist tea server attends tables in the traditional manner. 🚇 Tsim Sha Tsui, Map p.303 F2 **78**

The Lobby
The Peninsula Hong Kong

International
2920 2888

Don't miss the colonial-styled Lobby restaurant of the Peninsula Hotel. This 1920s styled restaurant dominates the ground floor, with chandeliered ceilings, thick rugs and white marbled floors. Conversations are moderated by the constant buzz of hotel guests and the strains of a live string band from the balcony above. With its international list of light meals, most diners come for the traditional high tea. Simply spiffing! 🚇 Tsim Sha Tsui, Map p.302 C4 **79**

Main St. Deli
Langham Hotel

American
2375 1133

Islanders regularly cross the harbour just to sample this New York-style deli's American fare. Choose from burgers, bagels, soups and hot sandwiches, including the house speciality – the Reuben: corned beef, pastrami, sauerkraut and melted Swiss cheese on toasted rye bread. Ingredients are flown directly from New York and the portions are massive. With its black and white floor tiles, art deco fixtures and chandeliers, everything is sparkling clean and welcoming.

Tsim Sha Tsui, Map p.302 B3 **80**

The Mistral
InterContinental Grand Stanford

Italian
2731 2870

Buried beneath the InterContinental in Kowloon lies The Mistral, a restaurant decorated to resemble a rustic Italian country home with tiled floors, stucco walls, and low wooden beams. Low lighting, well-spaced tables and a talented, wandering troubadour ensure a cosy atmosphere. The Mistral's menu features ample portions of various classic Italian dishes and an extensive wine selection. The music creates a fun atmosphere suitable for a group night out or relaxed date. Tsim Sha Tsui, Map p.303 F2 **81**

SPOON
InterContinental Hong Kong

Fine Dining
2313 2256

For a restaurant conceptualised by Alain Ducasse, one of the world's most Michelin star-decorated chefs, the staff here is surprisingly down-to-earth and go out of their way to ensure your experience is exquisite. After marvelling over the adventurous Asian tinged French menu you may opt for one of the tasting menus. Between courses, languish in the lounge-like atmosphere and neutral-toned decor, absorb the breath-taking Victoria Harbour view, and contemplate the 554 glass spoons suspended from the ceiling. 🚇 Tsim Sha Tsui, Map p.303 D4 **82**

The Swiss Chalet
European
12-14 Hart Ave
2191 9197

Tucked away on Hart Avenue, this faux chalet is a favourite amongst the Swiss, German and Austrian expats. As the name suggests, the interior is fitted with lots of wood, faux windows with net curtains and an alpenhorn. The carefully prepared menu features Swiss classics and nightly specials with a few varieties of the all-too-popular fondue. A rarity in Hong Kong, the spotless Swiss Chalet serves Swiss wine, which is surprisingly good. 🚇 Tsim Sha Tsui, Map p.303 D2 **83**

Tsui Hang Village Restaurant
Chinese
Miramar Ctr, 132 Nathan Rd
2376 2882

It's easy to see why Tsui Hang has a loyal following. This spacious branch cleverly combines modern and traditional decor, with lattice screens, sleek wooden furniture and contemporary Chinese artwork. The menu offers basic Cantonese fare, along with some fancier dishes. Favourites include deep-fried crispy chicken with steamed garoupa. On weekends, this place teems with families treating themselves. The prices reflect the quality at Tsui Hang –it's money well spent, no doubt. 🚇 Tsim Sha Tsui, Map p.302 C1 **84**

Tutto Bene
7 Knutsford Terrace

Italian
2316 2116

Black and white photographs dot the warm yellow walls while couples whisper sweet nothings and small groups practice the fine art of conversation. Even with seating for around 100, both indoors and outdoors, the candlelit restaurant still seems cosy. The menu is traditional Italian and the presentation has a rustic simplicity, with the focus on freshness, texture and flavour. Dishes here out-class those of the more expensive restaurants. 📍 Tsim Sha Tsui, Map p.303 D1 85

Woodlands
Mirror Tower, 61 Mody Rd

Indian
2369 3718

A favourite among the Indian community, this simple restaurant has no decor except for a couple of posters declaring vegetarianism ideals. People come to Woodlands for the tooth-suckingly good, authentic vegetarian cuisine. Central to the restaurant's enduring success are the thalis – choose from Bathura, Puree or Chapatti. Woodlands doesn't hold an alcohol license, but it does a mean mango lassi and has a selection of Indian soft-drinks. You'd be hard pushed to find a better dish for your dollar. 📍 Tsim Sha Tsui, Map p.303 E2 86

Bars & Pubs

8 Fine Irishmen
8 Observatory Rd

Pub
2316 2133

Stout on tap and traditional, hearty pub grub. Your favourite classic brews are all on the menu as well as large portions of fish and chips, shepherd's pie and the like. Make this your first port of call before a night of pub trawling, as it's small and quickly gets packed and noisy. There are a few dining tables available, but they get filled quickly and you may have to stand or opt for the less comfortable high tables with stools. Sound familiar? 🔲 Tsim Sha Tsui, Map p.303 E1 **87**

Aqua Spirit
One Peking Rd

Bar
3427 2288

The view here is surely the best in town and could not fail to impress even the most jaded Hong Konger. Add to that the super sexy decor, an extensive, albeit pricey, drinks list and great tunes and you're onto a winner. You can also enjoy excellent Italian and Japanese food in the restaurants just below the bar. Don't miss the Bollywood Nights when a bejewelled Indian crowd flock to shake their things to Bangra beats. 🔲 Tsim Sha Tsui, Map p.302 C3 **88**

Bahama Mama's Caribbean Bar
4-5 Knutsford Terrace

Bar
2638 2121

Bahama Mama's may not impress style junkies, but then it's not trying to. Instead it offers a laid back slice of tropical paradise right on one of Kowloon's busiest food streets. The palm trees, fairy lights and ceiling-suspended row boat read West Indies beach bar. Warm and friendly staff go out of their way to make customers feel comfortable and at home. A fairly typical list of tasty bar snacks is available, and portions are generous. 🔲 Tsim Sha Tsui, Map p.303 D1 **89**

Wan Chai

True, its reputation may precede it, but Wan Chai is not all about girly bars and naughty boys. There are some top restaurants and classy bars to be found.

Fancy being transported to Bali, without paying the air fare? Bebek Bengil 3 will take you there. Or perhaps you feel the need for speed and want to park yourself with the Porsche drivers at Fook Lam Moon? Whatever you're after, Wan Chai will make sure it happens.

Venue Finder

Restaurants

American Peking Restaurant
Chinese
20 Lockhart Rd
2527 1000

This place is an institution. In the 50s it attracted American GIs looking for tasty Chinese food and cheap beer, hence the name. The Beijing-style food is delicious and the perfect introduction to Chinese cuisine – not too heavy on the sea slugs. The sizzling prawns, chilli beef and peking duck especially stand out. The decor is basic and the atmosphere casual, with noisy chatter coming from diners at the large round tables. Waiters are brisk and sometimes a trifle brusque in true Hong Kong style. 🚇 Wan Chai, Map p.293 D4 **90**

Bebek Bengil 3
Indonesian
The Broadway, 54-62 Lockhart Rd
2217 8000

With its fantastic outdoor lesehan (raised floor seating), traditional teak wood interior, running fountains, servers in traditional garb and evocative gamelan music, this is as close as you can get to the magical island of Bali without getting on a plane. Then there is the food: a collection of traditional Balinese dishes prepared and served in creative ways. For example, the fish skewers are served on a tiny barbecue with hot coals. All the food here is good, but nothing beats abandoning cutlery to get stuck into their signature crispy duck with your hands.

🚇 Wan Chai, Map p.293 E4 **91**

Cine Citta
G/F 9 Star St

Italian

2529 0199

With the freshest pasta in Hong Kong, Italian movie star glamour, and waiting staff who talk you through the menu, Cine Citta is uber-cool. It's ideal for a business lunch, a date or a meal with friends. Sample the antipasto with some wine from the enormous glass cellar, the restaurant's centrepiece. The cuisine is modern Italian, featuring a wide range of meat and seafood mains, risottos and original pastas. Food is served against the backdrop of red velvet curtains, stills of Italian movie stars and Italian cinema classics screened to club-beats and chillout tunes. No carbonara or bolognaise here.

Wan Chai, Map p.299 D1 92

Fook Lam Moon
35-45 Johnston Rd

Chinese

2866 0663

You'll spot FLM by the Porsches and Ferraris parked outside. The spacious interior and understated beige and gold decor promote a relaxing atmosphere, and the food is traditional Cantonese of the highest order. Specialities include shark's fin, abalone and bird's nest together with a range of more standard dishes. Of course this kind of quality comes at a cost, so visit after a successful night at the races.

Wan Chai, Map p.299 E1 93

Khana Khazana
Dannies House, 20 Luard Rd

Indian

2520 5308

Indian regulars watching international cricket, and simple furnishings can only mean one thing – good, cheap Indian food. One floor above the busy streets of Wan Chai, this Indian vegetarian restaurant serves tasty dishes on silver platters amidst non-stop Hindi music. The daily $88 lunch buffet is a great bargain, offering salads, starters, vegetables and dal. Stick to the southern Indian specialties no matter how irresistible the Asian, Italian and Mexican dishes may seem.

🌐 Wan Chai, Map p.293 E4 94

One Fifth Grill
9 Star St

European
2529 6038

Forget the hype surrounding OFG, the reality is you will be served quality European food prepared by world class chefs. The restaurant's design is a modern take on a medieval banquet hall with reddy browns and candle-inspired lighting. The chic eatery attracts a trendy, self-conscious crowd who know good food when they see it. Chef Daniel Brolese insists the crispy duck leg is directly imported from France, and the dark, rich flavours of the 'Chocolate Fantasy' will truly dazzle. As you would expect from such a place, the wine menu is first class and handpicked to complement the food.

🌐 Wan Chai, Map p.299 D1 92

Quanjude
China Resources Bld, 26 Harbour Rd

Chinese
2884 9088

With no outdoor sign, few people know about Quanjude. However, it's one of the city's most authentic and delicious dining experiences. As you walk into the vast, gaudily decorated room, the clatter of crockery and Cantonese chatter greet you. Try the roast peking duck – imported from

Beijing and roasted 'imperial style'. Carved up at your table within minutes, roll a few succulent morsels in a pancake with some crispy cucumber, spring onion and sweet plum sauce. Heaven. 🚇 Wan Chai, Map p.293 F4 **96**

Quarterdeck Club
Australian

Fenwick Pier, 1 Lung King St
2827 8882

This is one of the few restaurants to offer comfortable outdoor seating by the harbour – in spite of the blighted view from the land reclamation work site. Inside, it's spacious, child-friendly and relaxed with a maritime theme. The menu has a distinctly American bent, despite claiming to be Australian. Expect standards such as sandwiches, pizzas and burgers served in big portions. Best to take a cue from the setting and stick with fish. The extensive seafood platter is enough to share. The bill takes a bite out of the wallet, so wait for a clear day and hearty appetite. 🚇 Wan Chai, Map p.293 D3 **97**

The Viceroy
Indian

Sun Hung Kai Ctr, 30 Harbour Rd
2827 7777

Master of reinvention, The Viceroy has survived for years. The quintessential Indian restaurant, on the harbour front of Wan Chai, has a large outside area to make full use of its gorgeous harbour views. The cavernous interior is full of polished woods, while outside boasts lush tropical plants, Hindu statues and wooden decking. The clientele is mainly well-to-do Indian families, with a few Europeans and local Chinese filling the gaps. The scrumptious food is Indian, with the recent addition of a small Middle Eastern menu. The Viceroy is also a premier stand-up comedy spot, with shows on Fridays or Saturdays. 🔲 Wan Chai, Map p.294 A3 98

Bars & Pubs

Chinatown
Bar
78-82 Jaffe Rd
2861 3588

This is a novel concept – a bar that's actually in China, but looks like a bar in New York pretending to be a bar in China. Chinatown takes faux Chinese to a new level. The deep green and bright red colour scheme is reminiscent of the rickshaws that now sit out of action at the star ferry. Plaster dragons, Chinese pop art and a giant fan decorate the walls while huge red lanterns hang from the ceiling. The drinks list is rather unadventurous and it's clear from the bellies walking around that most of the clientele are beer drinkers. Pub grub is served as well as a roast on Sundays, and on Tuesdays there's a quiz night. 🔲 Wan Chai, Map p.293 E4 99

Coyote Bar and Grill
Bar
114-120 Lockhart Rd
2861 2221

Live entertainment, a busy bar area and a huge margarita menu impart the desired Latin vibe. Alongside the standard Tex-Mex menu, Coyote's offers daily grilled specials of seafood and steak and massive Mexican brunches on weekends. Diners seated upstairs can keep an eye on the band and the bar, where enthusiastic patrons lean backwards over the counter to 'sample' the largest selection of tequila and mescal in Asia. 🔊 Wan Chai, Map p.293 E4 **100**

Klong
Bar

The Broadway, 54-62 Lockhart Rd   2217 8330

A largish bar overlooking Lockhart Road, Klong takes on several forms. One invites lounging with low tables and Thai cushions, while another encourages bird-like voyeurism from high tables overlooking the street below. Still another houses a pool table and dance floor, above which is a small platform and a solitary pole. With the growing popularity of pole dancing lessons, it's not unusual to see some lithe young thing pulling off her new, professional-looking moves. 🔊 Wan Chai, Map p.293 E4 **91**

Nightclubs

JJ's
Nightclub

Grand Hyatt Hong Kong   2584 7662

Part restaurant, part bar, part club, JJ's has something for everyone. The restaurant on the lower level serves 'six star Thai cuisine', with such innovative offerings as taro fritters with a tamarind dipping sauce and warm dark chocolate chilli tartelette with mango sherbet. Upstairs there are two bar areas and the legendary Music Room where a live band plays R&B nightly to a receptive crowd. Although JJ's is rather swanky and the drinks prices are on the high side, it's pleasantly unpretentious. One point to note – the air-conditioning is on overdrive, so bring an extra layer.

🔊 Wan Chai, Map p.293 E3 **102**

Joe Banana's

Nightclub

23 Luard Rd

2529 1811

For 20 years Joe Banana's has been the undisputed epicentre of Wan Chai nightlife. If you haven't pulled by 04:00, then this is the place to come. The mere mention of JBs makes many people cringe as they remember bad chat up lines, unfortunate dance moves and ill-advised pick ups. There are occasional live bands but at other times the DJ pumps out chart toppers and golden oldies that get the crowd going. Brave the dance floor only if you don't mind being groped. The crowd is mixed and includes tourists, air crew, US marines and ladies of questionable repute. It may be on the seedy side but it's all good fun. ⊞ Wan Chai, Map p.293 E4 103

One Fifth Ultralounge

Nightclub

9 Star St

2520 2515

One Fifth is the venue that first put the twinkle in Star Street. Although it may be past its hey day, it remains popular and you may even have to queue on a busy night. Once inside, a narrow corridor with a mirrored ceiling opens into the large, uber-chic bar. The high ceilings and lashings of metal give an industrial feel, while chocolate brown velour lounge areas add glam. Behind the long bar, drinks are stacked two metres high. You name it, it's on the menu, but cosmopolitans seem to be de rigueur. Resident DJs spin funk and soul – loudly – and despite the lack of a dance floor, people still seem to get down. One Fifth attracts a young, beautiful, ABC crowd. ⊞ Wan Chai, Map p.299 D1 92

Further Out

Take a trip up The Peak, over to Lantau Island, or just head somewhere different for a tasty bite while out shopping in Langham Place.

This short section suggests a few venues outside the areas already covered. During your time in Hong Kong you should certainly take a trip to the top of The Peak. While you're at the top, Café Deco and Peak Lookout offer different dining experiences, but one thing they have in common is the spectacular views. If you find yourself over in Whampoa Gardens, then Japanese restaurant Robatayaki comes highly recommended, although the prices are not for the feint-hearted. Langham Place in Mong Kok is a shopper's paradise, and Funky Fish and Ming Ya Fe should revive the weariest of bargain hunters. And finally, The Stoep on Lantau Island is one of those places you'll wish you could visit over and over again.

Venue Finder

Restaurants

Café Deco
International

The Peak Galleria, 118 Peak Rd   2849 5111

Café Deco is a huge two-floor restaurant on the Peak, with
a grand spiral staircase and floor to ceiling windows. Its
main draw is the view over Hong Kong, best enjoyed on
a clear evening. Despite Café Deco's efforts, the sheer size
of this place detracts from the atmosphere, although they
excel at serving a huge range of dishes to a huge number of
people. The menu is truly international, and the food doesn't
disappoint. Map p.296 B3 **105**

Funky Fish
Japanese

Langham Place   2782 6886

Funky Fish offers cheap and decent Japanese food and a
pleasant environment in which to take a break from shopping.
The design is fairly minimalist, with light wood and soft tones.
The atmosphere is relaxed and the service is excellent. The
extensive menu features all the usual favourites from sushi to
ramen and tempura. All the dishes are fresh, tasty and come in
decent portions. 🚇 Mong Kok, Map p.306 B2 **106**

Ming Ya Fe
Chinese

Langham Place   2782 2200

This Langham Place eatery serves tasty Shanghainese
fusion style food and also houses a lively bar. Although the
restaurant is of an open design, the careful lighting and rich
red tones lend a comfortable and intimate feel. The menu has

plenty of choices for all palates, and though serving sizes are generally modest, flavour is plentiful and the presentation appealing. There is live music every night from around 21:00.

Mong Kok, Map p.306 B2 **106**

Peak Lookout
International

121 Peak Rd
2849 1000

Nestled in foliage next to the Peak Tram, the Peak Lookout occupies a charming colonial building. Seats on the terrace under the banyan trees offer fantastic views, and inside there are oyster and drinks bars as well a spacious dining area. Gentle live music and the sound of the trickling fountain are perfect accompaniments to the impeccable food and service. The cuisine is international, with a huge choice of Asian and European dishes, barbequed treats and tea time goodies.

Map p.296 B3 **105**

Robatayaki
Japanese

Harbour Plaza, Whampoa Gardens
2996 8438

Robatayaki offers traditional Japanese barbecue – you choose the delicacies you want and expert chefs grill them for you. Most of the action happens around the central barbecue where there's room for a dozen people to watch chefs do their thing. The menu offers an array of ingredients to throw on the grill, including crab, snapper and kobe beef. There's also superb sushi and sashimi. Prices can climb to dizzying heights, but the quality makes it all worthwhile. Map p.289 D1

Café Deco

The Stoep

African
2980 2699

32 Lower Cheung Sha Village

If Lantau is your destination, there's no finer place to eat than The Stoep. It's South African-owned, so expect authentic native dishes. The legendary home-made bread is perfect to mop up tasty dips before moving on to the meaty mains. Step off the sand onto the covered terrace, and prepare to lounge away the hours in wicker chairs. The atmosphere here is strictly casual – you'll feel overdressed in anything but shorts. Indeed, many of the diners have just swum in from junks moored in the bay – sopping wet is a perfectly acceptable style at The Stoep. Map p.286 B4

Entertainment

From cheap and cheerful to the more extravagant, Hong Kong's cabaret, theatre, cinema and comedy options are worth sampling while you're in town.

Cabaret & Strip Shows

Despite the impression you might get walking around Wan Chai, the strip club scene in Hong Kong is pretty tame. So much so that most punters head to Macau for their fix of gyrating topless girls and cheap thrills. Here in Hong Kong the girls in most girly bars are merely scantily dressed rather than topless or nude. This doesn't stop owners charging hugely elevated prices for drinks though, and it's all still a little seedy. One possible exception to the rule is Goodfellas (2522 9218), a slightly better than average club on Ice House Street (map p.291, E-4). There is a hefty membership fee and drinks are still pricey after that. However, the western girls do full stripteases and lap dances. And just in case anyone's interested, some of them really can dance.

Cinemas

There are more than 40 cinemas in Hong Kong, ranging from small two-screen operations to multi-screen complexes. You can find a cinema in most areas, and in busy shopping areas like Tsim Sha Tsui and Causeway Bay you are spoilt for choice. The majority of films are English language or Cantonese. All English language films are subtitled in

Hong Kong Cinemas

AMC Festival Walk	Kowloon Tong	2265 8933
AMC Pacific Place	Admiralty	2265 8933
Broadway Cinematheque	Yau Ma Tei	2388 0002
Chinachem Golden Plaza	Tsim Sha Tsui	2311 3004
Cine Art House	Wan Chai	2827 4820
Golden Harvest Golden Gateway	Tsim Sha Tsui	2956 2003
Golden Harvest Grand Ocean	Tsim Sha Tsui	2377 2100
Golden Harvest Hollywood	Wong Tai Sin	2955 5266
Golden Harvest Mong Kok	Mong Kok	2628 9864
Golden Harvest New York	Causeway Bay	2838 7380
Golden Harvest Tsing Yi	Tsing Yi	2186 1333
MCL JP	Causeway Bay	2881 5005
Olympian City	Mong Kok	2388 6268
Palace IFC	Central	2388 6268
UA Citygate	Lantau Island	2109 3568
UA Cityplaza	Taikoo Shing	2567 9669
UA Langham Place	Mong Kok	3514 9031
UA Telford	Kowloon Bay	2758 9997
UA Times Square	Causeway Bay	2506 2822
UA Whampoa	Hung Hom	2303 1041
Windsor Cinema	Causeway Bay	2577 0783

Chinese, and some are dubbed into Cantonese. If you're looking for films in other languages, such as French, German, Italian or Japanese, try Broadway Cinematheque in Yau Ma Tei or the Cine Art House in Wan Chai. Hong Kong films are usually censored for nudity or sex scenes while the swearing, violence and bloodshed remain untouched. All cinemas have modern sound systems which are usually a little on the loud side, and they also have powerful air-conditioning systems so take an extra layer. Ticket prices range from $40 to $80, with cheaper deals for lunchtime showings and special deals on Tuesdays at some venues. For a premier cinema experience try the Directors Club in UA Cityplaza, Taikoo Shing or the Palace in Windsor House, Causeway Bay. These offer seats for couples, along with complimentary food and soft drinks, a bar and a state of the art screen and sound system. The Hong Kong International film festival held in April showcases hundreds of films in cinemas all across the territory. To find cinema listings check the English language newspapers or entertainment magazines.

Comedy

The Punchline Comedy Club is the main purveyor of stand-up comedy in Hong Kong. Shows take place in the Viceroy restaurant, Wan Chai (p.254) and feature comedians from the UK, Ireland, and North America. These nights are very popular and always packed. The Viceroy offers a dinner buffet before the show to make a night of it. Tickets are around $290 and you can expect to see three or four acts. Be warned, these shows are for a mature audience so don't bring the kids. For details of upcoming dates visit the club's website, www.punchlinecomedy.com/hongkong. Alternatively the Fringe Club in Central (p.219) has been known to present the odd comedy act. Visit www.hkfringe.com.hk for details of upcoming shows.

Hong Kong Cultural Centre

Theatre

Hong Kong is not exactly renowned for its theatre. In fact, for many years decent English language productions were almost completely lacking. However, efforts are being made to change that. The yearly Arts Festival brings in a host of world class acts, from performances of Shakespeare to offerings from top Chinese directors. On occasion a West End hit even graces Hong Kong's shores. There's also a handful of local theatre groups, made up mainly of expats, that put on regular productions. Probably the best known and loved group is the Hong Kong Players (www. hongkongplayers.com). Their annual Christmas pantomime is an integral part of any Hong Kong Christmas.

香港文化中心
HONG KONG CULTURAL CENTRE

Profile

Culture

Don't be alarmed if you experience culture shock – things are just done a bit differently in Hong Kong.

People & Traditions

On arrival, Hong Kong looks like any modern city. But then you notice a local storekeeper lighting incense sticks at a little shrine outside his shop. Or that friends head out to lunch with their parents every Sunday. Or that you are gently scolded for not making eye contact. You'll still realise that despite outward appearances, many things work differently here.

The Confucian model still has a strong influence, with the family playing a very important part in local life; children often live at home into their twenties and thirties. The Chinese view of health will seem very different too, though most people (including doctors) see no conflict in using the best of western and traditional medicine remedies together. Visit a western doctor about flu, for example, and you are likely to leave with the usual medicines, plus instructions to buy a glass of hot cola with ginger.

And there are those beliefs that will seem superstitious to outsiders, but are strongly held by locals. Many place great faith in Feng Shui, for example, and consult a trusted master for advice on decisions from how to arrange furniture in a new house, to what day to marry. Business people have also been known to consult them about big decisions, or if they have been facing unexpected problems.

Tai Chi in Victoria Park

Food & Drink

Chinese food in Hong Kong will taste different from your local Chinese restaurant at home, which comes as a disappointment to some visitors. Once you get past this, Hong Kong's food is likely to be one of your happiest memories of your time here. The majority of Hong Kong's residents hail from the Guangdong (Canton) region of southern China, so naturally Cantonese food is the most widely available. Dim sum (also called yum cha) is a popular style of Cantonese food and should be tried. Its a kind of tapas of Chinese dumplings. Dim sum are served in small portions, in bamboo baskets if steamed, or on plates if fried or baked. It's available from early morning through to early

afternoon. Smaller 'hole-in-the-wall' restaurants serve other Cantonese food such as roast meat with rice, or steamed/ stewed food such as beef brisket or prawn dumplings served with noodles. Outside stalls, tend to offer just a couple of dishes such as beef balls with noodles. Then there are the street vendors, selling a variety of deep fried foods from their push carts. Many Hong Kong people swear by this snack food, but marinated pig's ear isn't everyone's taste. Tap water is perfectly drinkable.

Seafood

Seafood deserves a special mention, given Hong Kong's coastal location. Seafood restaurants in the city have large fish tanks installed, so you can point out your chosen dish as it swims past. It'll be whisked away for a rendezvous with a sharp knife and a hot wok, then return a few minutes later cooked to your taste. If you have time, skip the city restaurants and take a ferry to one of the restaurants on Cheung Chau or Lamma Island instead (see p.84). The surroundings are more basic, but the outdoor setting makes it well worth the trip.

Chopsticks

If you're relatively new to chopsticks you'll find you drop as much on the table as you get to your mouth. Persevere though; the extra reach makes it easier to grab what you want from across the table. You'll soon be moving slippery button mushrooms from dish to mouth without them pinging off into a neighbour's bowl.

Other Food

The staple grain of north China is wheat, unlike the rice that grows in the south. So with northern food you can expect more breads, pancakes and pastries. Peking Duck is an obvious example. Northern food also tends to use more chilli, with Szechuan dishes the most eye-watering. If you need a break from Chinese food there are plenty of other Asian countries' cuisines to try, from Japanese sushi to Nepalese water buffalo.

Western food is easy to find, but the choice of restaurants is small and the prices are high. McDonalds and KFC are found throughout the city. In the cheaper western restaurants be prepared for 'western' food that doesn't taste quite right, for example, Italian recipes which have been tweaked to match local tastes, just like Chinese food is at home.

Religion

Hong Kong residents are granted religious freedom by The Basic Law, and Hong Kong is very tolerant of different faiths. All major religions are represented here, with over 500,000 Christians, and strong Muslim, Hindu, Sikh and Jewish communities. Local religious practice is a mish-mash of Buddhism, Taoism, and ancestor worship. Hong Kong's temples often contain a mix of Buddhist and Taoist deities.

Although these temples are often busy with tourists, you'll find they are still in very active use. You'll see people making offerings of incense and burning paper 'money', hoping for good fortune in return. Many temples also offer fortune-telling services, through use of 'chim', ie. a cup filled with small numbered sticks that's shaken until one of the sticks falls out. The stick is then taken to a temple attendant, who gives you a copy of the fortune that matches your number. Hong Kong's long coastline means many local temples are dedicated to Tin Hau, the goddess protecting seafarers. Fishing villages typically had a temple to her, located on the seashore. Other popular local deities include Kwun Yum (the Buddhist Goddess of Mercy), Pak Tai (Supreme Emperor of the Dark Heaven and local patron of the island of Cheung Chau) and Hung Shing (God of the South Seas and a weather prophet).

Government & Politics

The structure of Hong Kong's government is defined in 'The Basic Law of the Hong Kong Special Administrative Region' (known as The Basic Law). This in turn follows the agreements reached between Britain and China prior to the 1997 handover. The key point of those agreements is summarized as 'one country; two systems', meaning that, for at least 50 years after the handover, China agrees that Hong Kong's previous capitalist system and lifestyle will be left untouched.

The head of the executive branch of Hong Kong's government is the Chief Executive (CE). The first CE, Tung Chee Hwa, resigned in 2005 part-way through his second term. His replacement, Sir Donald Tsang, completed the remainder of Tung's second term and was then re-elected in March 2007.

Hong Kong's civil service is considered competent and relatively free from corruption. Transparency International's Corruption Perceptions Index for 2005 ranks Hong Kong as the world's 15th least corrupt country, out of a total of 158.

The Legislative Council has the power to enact laws; examine and approve budgets, taxation and public expenditure and monitor the work of the government. The third and final branch of government is the judiciary. Hong Kong continues to follow the common law traditions established during British rule, and the strong rule of law is seen as one of Hong Kong's key attractions to businesses.

Who Rules Hong Kong?

The Basic Law states that the Beijing government is responsible for Hong Kong's defence and foreign affairs. But, importantly, it also notes that Hong Kong will enjoy 'executive, legislative and independent judicial power'. But when tough decisions must be made, politicians in Hong Kong look over their shoulders uneasily and ask, what will Beijing say?

History

Hong Kong is steeped in history. From its past as a haven for fishermen and farmers to a vital port for dynasties and empires, it is a place built on trade, war and enterprising immigrants.

The Distant Past

Archaeological studies show that parts of Hong Kong have been inhabited for at least five millennia. The area was incorporated into the Chinese empire in the Qin Dynasty, around 200BC. Ancient Hong Kong may originally have been a salt production and pearl fishing hub, but in the Tang Dynasty, around 1,000 years ago, trade took on a greater role. Hong Kong briefly played host to the court of the Southern Song Dynasty in the late 13th century, as the Mongols swept through China's northern reaches.

Contact with the West

The 16th century witnessed Hong Kong's growing contact with the west. Portuguese traders were the first to arrive, although they were expelled and eventually set up shop across the Pearl River delta in Macau. The British East India Company arrived in 1699, and trade with the British empire developed quickly. Hong Kong was mostly bypassed in favour of Canton (modern Guangzhou) during these years, however, leaving some fishing villages and quite a few pirates.

The Big Buddha

Modern Hong Kong

Modern Hong Kong is the offspring of the Opium War, fought between Britain and China between 1839 and 1842. Hong Kong island was ceded to the victorious British in the Treaty of Nanking. Another round of the Opium War broke out soon after, with a similar result: in 1860, under the Convention of Peking, the Kowloon Peninsula came under British rule. The New Territories were annexed via a 99-year lease in 1898, mostly to provide a defence buffer around the city. During this time, Hong Kong's rapidly expanding, trade-based economy fuelled the building of dockyards, warehouses and colonial villas. The population grew steadily, fed by a stream of migrant workers from Guangdong Province.

War, and More War

After a long and relatively peaceful phase of expansion, World War II threw Hong Kong into chaos. The Japanese launched an invasion across the mainland border just hours after their attack on Pearl Harbour and, despite the brave and desperate defence of its armed forces, Hong Kong could not offer long-term resistance. The city fell on Christmas day, 1941. The following years of occupation were bleak, with mass rapes, the imprisonment of westerners in concentration camps, and economic collapse. Many of Hong Kong's Chinese residents were forcibly repatriated. Hong Kong's population of 1.6 million at the start of the war was reduced to just 500,000 by its end. Hong Kong was finally returned to British control in August 1945, after the defeat of Japan.

The British government tried to stay neutral during the final phases of China's civil war, but the city's population was soon swelled by refugees escaping the 1949 communist victory. At this point, Chinese forces might easily have overrun Hong Kong, but the mainland believed it was better off leaving Hong Kong's valuable economy alone. Further waves of immigrants were set off by the Great Leap Forward in the late 50s, and the Cultural Revolution of the mid 60s.

The Lease Runs Out

The next few decades saw Hong Kong's economy grow at a furious pace, as it shifted from a manufacturing to a service based economy.

In 1982, talks on Hong Kong's future began between the UK and Chinese governments. Chinese leader, Deng Xiao Ping, stood firm: nothing would do but the transfer of all of Hong Kong. The British Government acknowledged that it would be futile to attempt to retain Kowloon or Hong Kong island independently of the New Territories.

In 1984 it was agreed that Hong Kong would become part of China under a 'one country; two systems' arrangement: that is, Hong Kong would retain its economic and social independence, and its common-law jurisprudence. Beijing's 1989 Tiananmen Square Massacre heightened tensions in Hong Kong, and spurred many people to emigrate. Nevertheless, the Basic Law, a mini constitution for post-handover Hong Kong, was approved in 1990, and the handover was completed on July 1, 1997.

Hong Kong Timeline

221BC	First mention of Hong Kong in Chinese records
16th century AD	Hong Kong comprises small villages; growing contacts with the west
1842	Treaty of Nanking cedes Hong Kong island to the British at conclusion of Opium War
1860	Convention of Peking adds the Kowloon peninsula to Hong Kong's territory
1899	The New Territories added via a 99-year lease
1920s	Period of unrest marked by Seamen's Strike in 1922
1941	Hong Kong falls to invading Japanese army
1945	Hong Kong returned to British rule after Japanese surrender
1950s	Waves of immigrants from mainland China swell Hong Kong's population; social services and public housing greatly expanded

1960s	Population continues to grow along with economy; communist-led riots break out in 1967
1984	British Prime Minister Margaret Thatcher and Chinese Premier Zhao Ziyang sign the Joint Declaration ensuring Hong Kong's return to Chinese sovereignty in 1997
1989	Tiananmen Square crackdown in Beijing sparks huge demonstrations in Hong Kong
1992-1995	Hong Kong's last Governor, Chris Patten, attempts to introduce democratic reforms, to decidedly mixed reactions
1997	Hong Kong handover
1997-2003	Deep recession and high unemployment
2003	SARS crisis, everyone in Hong Kong wearing surgical masks
2005	Tung resigns as popularity drops; cites health reasons. Donald Tsang is named to serve out the remainder of Tung's term

Hong Kong Today

Hong Kong has been in the spotlight for years and has come under close political scrutiny. Hasn't every city? As the economy continues to grow, it becomes an increasingly 'must visit' destination.

The Post-Handover Years

Tung Chee Hwa, a wealthy shipping magnate, was selected as Hong Kong's first Chief Executive. His term of office started relatively well, but his administration was dogged by the Asian financial crisis of the late 90s and a number of policy blunders. The 2003 SARS epidemic, which was centred in Hong Kong, was another significant setback. The massive pro-democracy march in Hong Kong on July 1, 2003 was widely seen as a vote of no confidence in Tung, but he stayed in office until tendering his resignation in March 2005.

Tung was replaced by his then Chief Secretary, Donald Tsang, who is known both for his trademark bow tie, and for his long career as a civil servant. Hong Kong's economy has grown strongly since the recession of the late 90s, and the 2003 SARS epidemic. In 2005, Hong Kong's per-capita GDP was estimated at US$37,400.

Trade

Throughout the first hundred years of British rule, trade with China was the bedrock of the local economy. Hong Kong's sheltered harbour and proximity to Canton (Guangzhou) placed it perfectly for handling the sea-bound trade between China and the rest of the world.

Trade is still an important part of the local economy: in 2005, Hong Kong was the world's second busiest container port (first place went to Singapore). The real threat to Hong Kong's trade, however, is the nearby mainland city of Shenzhen. It is currently the fourth biggest container port, and its combination of good location and lower handling fees have increased its container traffic at around 20% per year, compared to single digit increases for Hong Kong.

Integration with China

Each stage of Hong Kong's economic development can be linked to events in mainland China, and this will continue to be the pattern for the future. Hong Kong's role as a provider of value-added services will be challenged as China develops, with Shanghai a worthy competitor.

On the bright side, China's market for Hong Kong's services continues to expand, with the two economies growing ever more interconnected. A free trade agreement with China, and the Closer Economic Partnership Arrangement (CEPA), apply zero tariffs to all Hong Kong-origin goods and preferential treatment in 27 service sectors.

Hong Kong, along with the Macau Special Administrative Region, has also joined a new pan-Pearl River Delta trade block with nine Chinese provinces, which aims to lower trade barriers among members, standardise regulations, and improve infrastructure.

The Future

Hong Kong has endured a dramatic decade since the handover. The collapse of the Asian financial markets sent the economy into recession, SARS drove investors away in 2003, and bird flu had the world worried about a pandemic, with southern Asia at its core.

But, the next decade looks a little brighter. In the late 90s, a lot of Hong Kong firms moved to southern China to take advantage of cheaper labour, and money is now flowing back into the region. As investors grow confident that Beijing will remain hands off, more money is being spent on building the city skywards. The Union Square development above Kowloon MTR station will include the International Commerce Centre and when completed in 2010, it will be Hong Kong's tallest building. And tourism is on the up too. In 2005, over 23 million people visited Hong Kong, almost double the 13 million that visited in 2000. Most of this increase can be traced back to the Chinese government's decision to make it easier for its citizens to visit.

For all that it is an international city, Hong Kong's future will largely be determined by its relationship with the big, brooding brother to the north. As China's capitalist experiment becomes something of an economic miracle, Hong Kong is only likely to benefit. As it grew on the coattails of the British empire in the 19th century, so it will grow on the coattails of the economic superpower of the 21st century. The one potential hurdle is the growing demand for more democracy in Hong Kong. The world is yet to see how the Chinese react to that.

Clockwise from top left: Kowloon high rises, Mid-Levels seen from The Peak

Maps

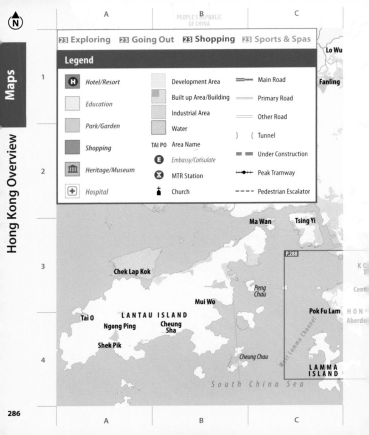

N

Sha Tau Kok

Lo Wu

anling

Plover Cove
Reservoir

Three Fathoms
Cove

Tai Po

Tolo
Harbour

Ma On
Shan

Sha Tin

Sai Kung

Kau
Sia Chau

High Island
Reservoir

KOWLOON
Tsim Sha
Tsui

Central Causeway
Bay

Clear Water Bay

HONG KONG ISLAND
Aberdeen

Fu Lam

Repulse
Bay

Sheck O

Stanley

MMA
AND

0 Scale 1:3,800 5km

PO TOI
ISLANDS

D   E   F

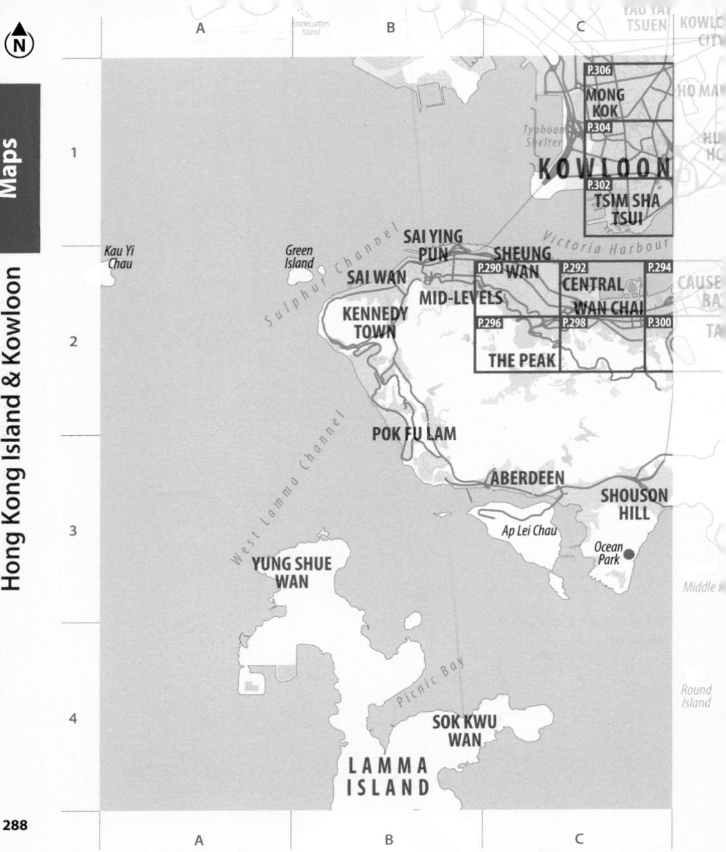
N
A
B
C
1
2
3
4
Stonecutters Island
TSUEN
KOWLOON CITY
P.306
MONG KOK
P.304
Typhoon Shelter
KOWLOON
P.302
TSIM SHA TSUI
Victoria Harbour
Kau Yi Chau
Green Island
Sulphur Channel
SAI YING PUN
SHEUNG WAN
SAI WAN
P.290
P.292
P.294
CENTRAL
WAN CHAI
MID-LEVELS
KENNEDY TOWN
P.296
P.298
P.300
THE PEAK
POK FU LAM
West Lamma Channel
ABERDEEN
SHOUSON HILL
Ap Lei Chau
Ocean Park
YUNG SHUE WAN
Picnic Bay
SOK KWU WAN
LAMMA ISLAND
Round Island

KOWLOON
CITY

Former
Hong Kong
International
Airport (Kai)

HO MAN TIN

NGAU TAU KOK

HANG HAU

Kowloon
Bay

HUNG
HOM

Oriental
Golf City

KWUN TONG

YAU TONG

TAI CHIK
CHAU

CAUSEWAY
BAY

LEI KING

Lei Yue Mun

SAI WAN HO

TAI HANG

Junk Bay

LEI YUE
MUN

Tai Tam
Reservoir

CHAI WAN

Ngan Wan

HONG KONG ISLAND

Big Wave Bay

REPULSE
BAY

Middle Island

SHECK O

Round
Island

Tai Tam Bay

STANLEY

D' AGUILAR
PENINSULA

Kau Pei
Chau

0   Scale 1:14,000   2km

Stanley Bay

STANLEY
PENINSULA

Beaufort
Island

Tsan Yuk Hospital

King George V Memorial Park

● Police Station

Tung Wah Hospital

Queen's St

Hollywood Rd

Bonham Str

Pa Yan St

Hospital Rd

Tai Ping Shan St

Lok Ku Rd

Bonham Rd

Pa Hing Fong

Po Hing Fong

Square St

Cat Street Bazaar 17

Man Mo Temple ● 5

🏛 Hong Kong Museum of Medical Sciences 3

Robinson Rd

Seymour Rd

MID-LEVELS

Shing Wong St

Bridges St

Aberdeen St

SOHO

Conduit Rd

Caine Rd

Corble Rd

Peel St

Mosque St

Mosque Jn

Robinson Rd

300 m

Lugard Rd

1000 ft

Sheung Wan ✦

Wing Lok St

Morrison St

Bonham Strand W

Burd St

Mercer St

Hillier St

Queen's Rd Central

Man Kwong St
Man Pa St
E
F
Pier 6
N

Finance St
Man Kwong St
Man Po St

11 H Four
Seasons

Wing On

Man Wu Ln
Rumsey St

Lok St
Wing Wo St

IFC Mall
3 22

Man Cheung St

TWO
IFC

17

Des Voeux Rd Central

Connaught Rd Central

9

Mercer St
Central

Jubilee St
Queen Victoria St

Harbour View St
E
Canada

Hong Kong

Mon Yiu St

Bus
Terminus

Exchange
Square

Gough St
26
16
33 24

Central
Market

Pottinger St
Li Yuen St W
21 Li Yuen St E

Connaught Pl

Hollywood Rd
Gage St

18

Cochrane St

23

Stanley St

Theatre Ln

292

2

Tourist
Information

Peel St
71

Graham St
Lyndhurst Ter

44

49

58

Pottinger St

Queens Rd

Chater House
13 Mandarin
Central Oriental

31

City Ha
CENT

Staunton St
64
60 67

52

Wellington St
Wo On Ln

19
37

D'Aguilar St

9

13

Pedder St
Landmark

Alexandra
House Prince's
Bldg

H

Ritz-Carlto
Hong Kong

Shelley St
Mid-Levels Escalator

Old Bailey St

Wing Wah Ln

16

Lan Kwai Fong

9
10

On Lan St
57

13 5

Duddell St

Landmark
Mandarin
Oriental H
51

HSBC
Bldg

Ice House St

Statue
Square

Chancery Ln

Caine Rd

Arbuthnot Rd

15
12

29 2

On Hing Ter

Glenealy

Hong Kong
Central Hospital H

7

Battery Path

Queensway

Bank of
China Tow

45

Upper Albert Rd

Government
House

Ice House St

Court of
Final Appeal

Bishop Lei H

Zoological &
Botanical
Gardens
9

Lower Albert Rd

USA
E
Garden Rd

Canossa
School

Albany Rd

297

Peak Tram Ter

300 m

1000 ft

Bank o
China Tow

Hong

D
E
F

291

Canossia
Hospital

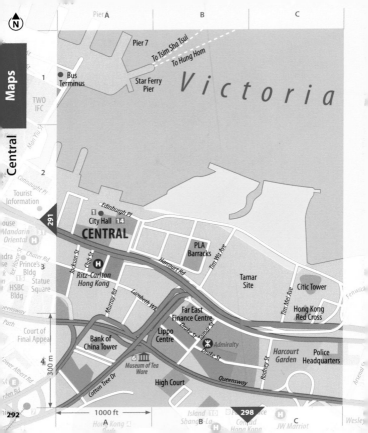

N

A

B

C

Pier A

Pier 7

To Tsim Sha Tsui

To Hung Hom

1

Bus Terminus

Star Ferry Pier

Victoria

TWO IFC

2

Tourist Information

Connaught Pl

Mon Yiu St

291

Edinburgh Pl

City Hall 14

CENTRAL

PLA Barracks

Tim Wa Ave

ouse

Mandarin Oriental

Chater Rd

andra se

Ice House St

Prince's Bldg

3

Ritz-Carlton Hong Kong

Ickson St

Club St

Harcourt Rd

Tamar Site

Citic Tower

Fenwick

HSBC Bldg

Statue Square

Murray Rd

Lambeth Wlk

Hong Kong Red Cross

ueensway

Path

Court of Final Appeal

Bank of China Tower

Far East Finance Centre

Lippo Centre

Drake St

Tamar St

Admiralty

Tim Mei Ave

4

300 m

6 Museum of Tea Ware

Cotton Tree Dr

Drake St

Queensway

Rodney St

Harcourt Garden

Police Headquarters

ower Albert Rd

en Rd

High Court

1000 ft

Island Shang B-La

298

Conrad

C

JW Marriott

Wesle

Harbour

D | E | F

97

Lung King St

Fenwick Pier St

Expo Drive

22 Hong Kong Convention & Exhibition Ctr

Expo Drive East

To Hung Hom

To Tsim Sha Tsui

294

Convention Ave

Convention Ave

Bus Terminus

Grand Hyatt
102

South Africa **E**

Australia & New Zealand **E**

Fleming Rd

Harbour Rd

Sun Hung Kai Centre

Tonnochy Rd

Hong Kong Academy for Performing Arts

HK Arts Centre **21**

Harbour Rd
YMCA Harbour View

Wan Chai Tower

WAN CHAI

Fenwick St

Telecom House

Revenue Tower

Central Plaza

96 China Visa Office

Immigration Tower

Gloucester Rd

Stewart Rd

Stewart Rd

China Fleet Club

Jaffe Rd

103

94

Belgian House

100

Jaffe Rd

Jaffe Rd

Police Station

Arsenal St

Lockhart Rd

90
Empire

99

Wharney **91**

New Harbour

Lockhart Rd

O'Brien Rd

Luard Rd

Fleming Rd

Lockhart Rd

Lockhart Rd

Century Hong Kong

299

Wesley

Anton St

Tonnochy Rd

Church

Wan Chai

Thomson Rd

Thomson Rd

Hennessy Rd

Burrows

300 m

1000 ft

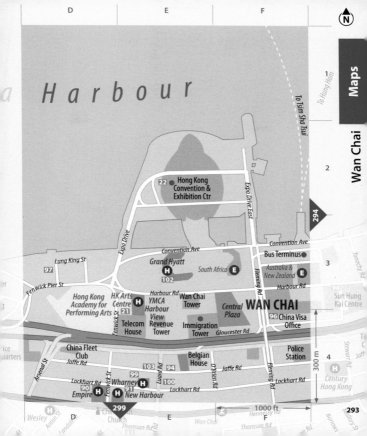

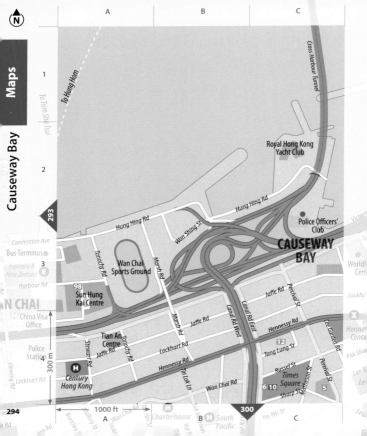

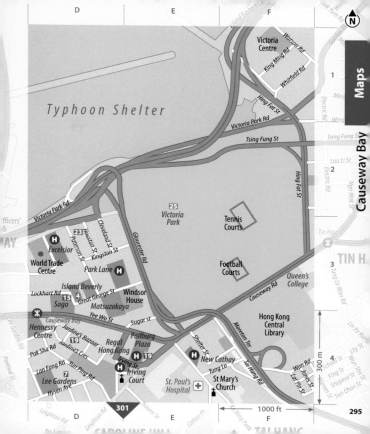

Causeway Bay

Typhoon Shelter

Victoria Centre

D E F

N

King Ming Rd

Watson Rd

Whitfield Rd

Hing Fat St

Victoria Park Rd

Tsing Fung St

Hing Fat St

Electric Rd

Wing

Tsing Fung St

Laa Li St

Electric Rd

Ngo Mok St

Tin Hau

TIN H.

Tung Lo Wan Rd

Victoria Park Rd

Cleveland St

Howloon St

Paterson St

Kingston St

Gloucester Rd

25 Victoria Park

Tennis Courts

Football Courts

Queen's College

H Excelsior

23

World Trade Centre

H Park Lane

Island Beverly

15 Sogo

Great George St

Windsor House

Matsuzakaya

Yee Wo St

Sugar st

Causeway Rd

Hong Kong Central Library

Lockhart Rd

Hennessy Centre

Jardine's Bazaar

19 Jardine's Cres

Pak Sha Rd

Lan Fong Rd

Yun Ping Rd

7 Lee Gardens

Hysen Ave

Regal Hong Kong

Pailburg Plaza

19 Irving St

Irving Court

St. Paul's Hospital

New Cathay

H

Shelter St

Moreton Ter

Tung Lo

St Mary's Church

Tai Hang Rd

Won Rd

Jones St

Lai Yin St

King St

Sheperd St

Sun Chun St

300 m

1000 ft

Lee Garden Rd

Percival St

Leighton Rd

Leighton Rd

Haven St

Cotton Pt

Yar Hing Path

301

CAROLINE HILL

TAI HANG

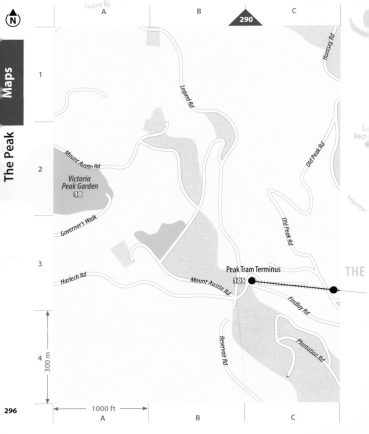

290

N

Lugard Rd

A

B

C

Hornsey Rd

1

Lugard Rd

Recr

2

Mount Austin Rd

Victoria
Peak Garden
10

Old Peak Rd

Tregunter

Governor's Walk

3

Harlech Rd

Mount Austin Rd
105

Peak Tram Terminus

Old Peak Rd

Findlay Rd

THE

Reservoir Rd

Phantation Rd

4

300 m

1000 ft

A

B

C

D | E | F

291

N

Zoological &
Botanical
Gardens

USA
Garden Rd

Hornsey Rd

Canossa
Hospital ✚

Robinson Rd

Garden Rd

Old Peak Rd

Peak Tram Terminus

7

St Josephs Path

Cotton Tree Drive

H
YWCA
Garden View

Calder Path

St Paul's
Co-Educ.
College

Macdonnell Rd

Macdonn

Ladies
Recreational
Club

May Rd

Brewin Path

Clovelly Pl

Police Station

Magazine Gap Rd

Bowen

2

298

Tregunter Path

May Rd

May Rd

Peak Tramway

THE PEAK

Barker Rd

3

Severn Rd

Severn Rd

Severn Rd

300 m

Pollock's Path

4

1000 ft

N

High Court

292

A

B

C

Wesley

Hong Kong
Park

Island
Shangri-La

Pacific Place

Conrad
Hong Kong

JW Marriott

10

H

H

H

Tien Poa St

Sun St

Sin Moon St

1

Supreme Court Rd

Justice Drive

Great Britain

E

Kennedy Rd

Macdonnell Rd

Borrett Rd

Kennedy

Police
Station

St Paul's
Educ.
College

Bowen Rd

Magazine Gap Rd

Borrett Rd

2

Bowen R

Island
School

297

Magazine Gap Rd

3

Barker Rd

Peak Rd

300 m

4

Magazine Gap Rd

Coomber Rd

Pollock's Path

Severn Rd

Rd

Police

1000 ft

A

B

C

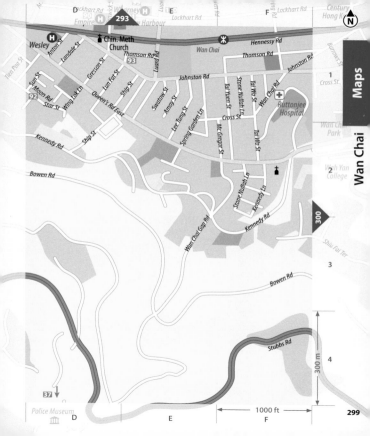

N

Century
Hong Kong

Lockhart Rd

Johnston Rd

A

B

Wan Chai Rd

294

C

Times
Square

Sharp St

Leig

Leig

Pe

Burrows St

Mallory St

Wan Chai Rd

Heard St

Tak Yan St

H Charterhouse

Lok Morrison Hill Rd

Yat Sin St

H South
Pacific

Yiu Wa St

Cross St

Wood Rd

Of Kwan Rd

Sung Tak St

Craigengower
Cricket Club

LEIGHTON
HILL

Stanjee
spital

Tang Shiu
Kn Hospital

Queen Elizabeth
Stadium

Canal Rd East

Sports Rd

Hong Kong
Jockey Club

Hong Kong
Football Club

Wong Nai Chung Rd

Wan Chai
Park

Queen's Rd East

1

Wah Yan
College

Khalsa Diwan
Sikh Temple

Hau Tak Ln

23

Hong Kong
Racing Museum

2

299

Muslim
Cemetery

HAPPY VALLEY

Rd

Shiu Fai Ter

Stubbs Rd

Roman
Catholic Cemetery

2

Happy Valley
Racecourse

3

Bowen Rd

Wong Nai Chung Rd

Stubbs Rd

Aberdeen Tunnel

Hindu Temple

4

300 m

Hong Kong
Sanatorium &
Hospital

Village Rd

Yik Yu
Shan Kwo

Yik Yu
Shan Kwo

300

1000 ft

Ig Kong
Academy

A

B

C

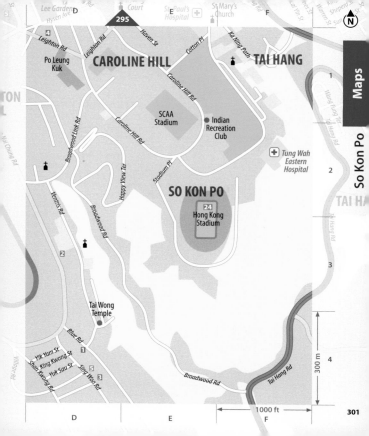

N

Austin Rd West

A

B

C

Victoria Towers

BP International H **304**

Police Station

Hillwc

St. A Cr

Obre

17 Kowloon Park

Park Lane Shopper's Boulevard

Nathan Rd

84

Mirama Centre

Kimbe

1

Royal Pacific **H**

TSIM SHA TSUI

Mir

China Ferry Terminal

Hong Kong Heritage Discovery Centre **12**

Cameror

Marco Polo Prince **H**

Kowloon Mosque

2 Harbour City

Halphong Rd

Tsim Sha Tsui

Humph

2

Carnarvon Rd

Silvercord

Ashley Rd

Hankow Rd

Lock Rd

Nathan Rd

Mirado Mansio

Marco Polo Gateway **H**

The Sun Arcade

Ichang St

Holiday Golden

Langham **H**

80

Park Drive

Peking Rd

88

Kowloon **H**

Imperia Middle

3

Middle Rd

Gateway Rd

Ocean Terminal

Marco Polo Hong Kong **H**

Star House

YMCA Salisbury **H**

Shanghai Tang

Peninsula

76 14

79

SI Ho Hote

Sag

Bus Terminus

Salisbury Rd Hong Kong Space Museum **16**

Tourist Information Office

11 Hong Kong Cultural Centre

Arts Library **13**

Star Ferry Pier

Clock Tower

To Central & Wan Chai

Hong Kong Museum of Art

300 m

1000 ft

302

A

B

C

Shenzhen

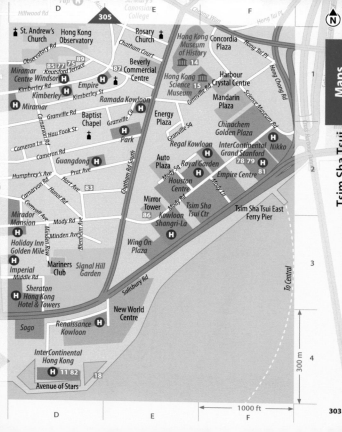

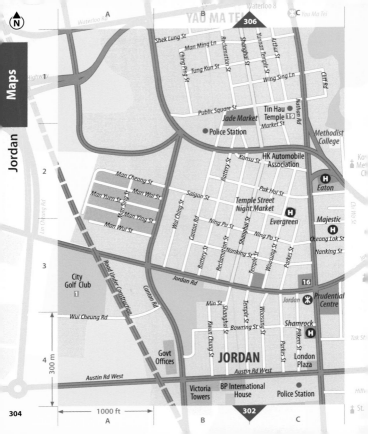

D | E | F

King's Park

307

Ui Man Shopping Centre

Estate

N

Chung Hau St

Chi Man St

1

King's Park Rise

Blood Transfusion Centre

British Military Hospital

Carmel English School

odist lege

Kowloon Methodist Church

Queen Elizabeth Hospital

South Kowloon Magistracy

Chi Wo St

Open University of Hong Kong

2

Wylie Rd

Wylie Path

Filipino Club

India Club

Wylie Path

Pakistan Club

estic

Diocesan Girls School

Lok St

ing St

Jordan Rd

Gasgoigne Rd

Girl Guides Assn

Jordan Path

United Services Recreation Club

Chatham Rd

3

Kowloon Union Church

ential tre

Car's Rd

Jordan Path

Gun Club Hill Barracks

Jordan Path

Yuk Choi Rd

Kowloon Cricket Club

Tak Shing St

Austin Rd West

Hong Kong Polytechnic University

300 m

4

Fuji H

Austin Ave

St. Mary's Canossian College

Cheong Wan

Hong Tai Pl

Hillwood Rd

St. Andrew's Church

Hong Kong Observatory

303

Rosary Church

Hong Kong Museum of History

Concordia Plaza

Ter

Rai Ter

1000 ft

305

D | E | F

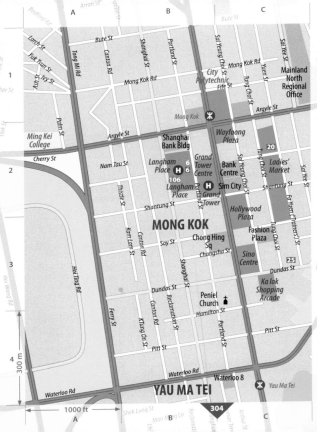

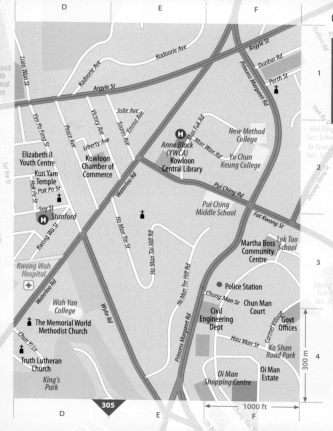

Mong Kok & Yau Ma Tei

Index

Explorer Products

Residents' Guides

All you need to know about living, working and enjoying life in these exciting destinations

 Abu Dhabi
 Amsterdam
 Bahrain

 Barcelona
 Dubai
 Dublin

 Geneva
 Hong Kong
 Kuwait

 London
 New York
 New Zealand
 Oman

 Paris
 Qatar
 Shanghai
 Singapore
 Sydney

* Covers not final. Titles available Winter 2007.

Mini Guides

Perfect pocket-sized
visitors' guides

 Abu Dhabi
 Amsterdam
 Bahrain

 Barcelona
 Dubai
 Dublin
 Hong Kong

 London
 New York
 New Zealand
 Oman

* Covers not
final. Titles
available
Winter 2007.

 Paris
 Shanghai
 Singapore
 Sydney

Activity Guides

Drive, trek, dive and swim... life will never be boring again

 off-road UAE
 off-road Oman
 trekking Oman
 underwater UAE

Mini Maps

Fit the city in your pocket

* Covers not final. Titles available Winter 2007.

Maps

Wherever you are, never get lost again

* Cover not final.

Photography Books

Beautiful cities caught through the lens.

Lifestyle Products & Calendars

The perfect accessories for a buzzing lifestyle

Explorer Team

Publisher
Alistair MacKenzie

Editorial
Managing Editor Claire England
Lead Editors David Quinn,
Jane Roberts, Matt Farquharson,
Sean Kearns, Tim Binks, Tom Jordan
Deputy Editors Helen Spearman,
Jake Marsico, Katie Drynan,
Richard Greig, Tracy Fitzgerald
Editorial Assistants Grace Carnay,
Ingrid Cupido, Mimi Stankova

Design
Creative Director Pete Maloney
Art Director Ieyad Charaf
Senior Designers Alex Jeffries,
Iain Young
Layout Manager Jayde Fernandes
Designers Hashim Moideen,
Rafi Pullat, Shefeeq Marakkatepurath,
Sunita Lakhiani
Cartography Manager
Zainudheen Madathil
Cartographer Noushad Madathil
Design Admin Manager
Shyrell Tamayo
Production Coordinator
Maricar Ong

IT
IT Administrator Ajay Krishnan
Senior Software Engineer
Bahrudeen Abdul
Software Engineer Roshni Ahuja

Photography
Photography Manager
Pamela Grist
Photographer Victor Romero
Image Editor Henry Hilos

Sales and Marketing
Area Sales Manager Stephen Jones
Marketing Manager Kate Fox
Retail Sales Manager
Ivan Rodrigues
Retail Sales Coordinator
Kiran Melwani
Corporate Sales Executive
Ben Merrett
Digital Content Manager
Derrick Pereira
Distribution Supervisor
Matthew Samuel
Distribution Executives
Ahmed Mainodin, Firos Khan,
Johny Mathews, Mannie Lugtu
Warehouse Assistant Mohammed
Kunjaymo, Najumudeen K.I.
Drivers Mohammed Sameer,
Shabsir Madathil

Finance and Administration
Administration Manager
Andrea Fust
Financial Manager Michael Samuel
Accounts Assistant Cherry Enriquez
Administrators Enrico Maullon,
Lennie Mangalino
Driver Rafi Jamal

Contact Us

▶ Reader Response
If you have any comments and suggestions, fill out
our online reader response form and you could win prizes.
Log on to **www.explorerpublishing.com**

▶ General Enquiries
We'd love to hear your thoughts and answer any questions
you have about this book or any other Explorer product.
Contact us at **info@explorerpublishing.com**

▶ Careers
If you fancy yourself as an Explorer, send your CV (stating the
position you're interested in) to **jobs@explorerpublishing.com**

▶ Designlab and Contract Publishing
For enquiries about Explorer's contract publishing arm and
design services contact **designlab@explorerpublishing.com**

▶ Maps
For cartography enquries, including orders and comments,
contact **maps@explorerpublishing.com**

▶ Corporate Sales
For bulk sales and customisation options, for this book or any
Explorer product, contact **sales@explorerpublishing.com**

Special thanks to our contributing authors: David Bellis, Freya
Simpson Giles, Lesley Croft, Paul Kay, Pete Spurrier, Ross Vermeer,
Victoria Burrows. Photographers: Pamela Grist, Pete Maloney,
David Quinn, Tom Jordan.

EXPLORER